Automobile Workers
and
the American Dream

AUTOMOBILE WORKERS
AND
THE AMERICAN DREAM

By ELY CHINOY, *Smith College*

Introduction by DAVID RIESMAN

BEACON PRESS   BOSTON

To

MY MOTHER AND FATHER

Acknowledgments

Sociological investigation rests fundamentally upon men's willingness to talk freely about themselves to researchers who usually can give nothing in return except their willingness to listen. My prime debt is to those automobile workers about whom this book is written. Without their cooperation the research could not have been done. They welcomed me into their homes and they gave generously of their time. Their answers to my questions constitute the core of this book.

I am also deeply grateful to the officers of the local union to which most of these men belonged and to several of its most active members. They encouraged workers to talk freely with me; they provided information about themselves, the union, and the factory; and in several instances they offered companionship and friendship which made easier and pleasanter this venture into a community in which I was a stranger. The need to maintain the anonymity of men who talked openly about themselves and, on occasion, about others, precludes identification of those to whom I am most indebted.

Victor Reuther, formerly Education Director of the United Automobile Workers and now administrative assistant to the president of the Congress of Industrial Organizations, helped to enlist the cooperation of local union officers; his assistance is gratefully acknowledged. I also wish to thank the executives who answered my questions about the organization and policies of the plant whose workers were interviewed, and the school officials and teachers who made it possible to secure information about the job aspirations of students in the high schools of "Autotown."

I owe more to Professor Robert S. Lynd for his continual encouragement, stimulation, and criticism than any acknowledgment can indicate. From the very inception of the investigation, I have drawn freely upon his aid. I am also grateful to Professor Robert K. Merton for counsel during most of the field work and for comments and suggestions at various stages in the analysis of the data and the preparation of the manuscript. My intellectual indebtedness to both of these men, however, goes far beyond their specific contributions to this book. Professors Seymour M. Lipset and Paul Brissenden read the manuscript critically. Professor Charles H. Page gave freely of himself both as colleague and editor.

My wife, Helen Krich Chinoy, has been a constant and indispensable aide and critic.

The bulk of the field work upon which this book is based was made possible by a Fellowship of the Social Science Research Council, to whom acknowledgment is gratefully made.

I wish to thank the following publishers for permission to quote from copyright material: Doubleday and Company, Inc., for a quotation from Alfred P. Sloan, *Adventures of a White Collar Man*, copyright by Alfred P. Sloan, Jr. and Boyden Sparks (1940, 1941); Oxford University Press for a quotation from C. Wright Mills, *White Collar* (1951); Harper and Brothers for material originally included in my article "Local Union Leadership," which appeared in *Studies in Leadership*, edited by Alvin W. Gouldner (1950); and the University of Chicago Press for material which first appeared in my article, "The Tradition of Opportunity and the Aspirations of Automobile Workers," in the *American Journal of Sociology* (May, 1952).

ELY CHINOY

Northampton, Mass.
January, 1955

Contents

List of Tables

Introduction

Ely Chinoy's book illustrates one of the salient "growth situations" in sociology. He starts with a big idea, one which has long occupied American social scientists, the idea of the American dream of equal opportunity for all. He circles around this idea in his first chapter, drawing on Horatio Alger and the autobiographies of men like Alfred P. Sloan, reminding us of how pervasive has been the ideology that success will come to those who will it. He raises, though he does not answer, the more skeptical questions of our own day: whether it was ever really so, in the internal frontiers of our cities, and whether it is less so now, even though, despite the more rigid structure of large organizations, some men can still "run around end" into small business (or union leadership positions) or can educate their offspring to enter large business and the service trades and professions. Then, to explore concretely the role of the American dream, he takes us to the auto industry as the epitome of the success story, a place where Scandinavian immigrants or "Scotch-Irish" natives could rise, if not quite from floor-sweeper, at least from pattern-making or machining to production boss. (He does not tell us—no one does, so far as I know—what sorts of models these mobile men saw about them in their youth, or what sorts of lessons in command they had, that made these careers possible; certainly, not all ethnic stocks participated.) He sketches the "career" of the auto industry itself, showing that today, as in other large manufacturing companies, it is rare and difficult to attain middle-class status through promotion from the bench. Wages in the industry, though high, are compressed in range, with 50 per cent of the workers earning within 14 cents an hour of each other. It is harder to start in today as a parts supplier than it once was to found Oldsmobile or Reo.

But while all this has been happening, Chinoy suggests that other changes have taken place in the values of American society. For example, success at one's job may increasingly be thought less important than "success" in one's general style of life, at home and off the job. The worker we shall quote later on who sees himself as "getting ahead" because he is working towards a "nice little modern house"; the other workers who, by securing a less demanding but equally well-paying job, preserve their energies for leisure; indeed, the whole group of workers for whom the fight for "fringe benefits" replaces the struggle for individual advance—all these, Chinoy's work indicates, respond by altered goals to altered possibilities. One great virtue of his book is that he presents this as a process in the life-cycle of the auto worker, who begins in high school with limited aspirations, learns some others in the plant, and surrenders still others as time goes by. We all do this, of course, but the auto worker would seem to give up taking his dreams seriously at an earlier point, so that, in terms of "set," he is an old man by his mid-thirties.

Chinoy's view of such outcomes has been greatly influenced by European and American discussions of "alienation." If he does not trace all evil to the bosses' exploitation, he does see the factory as the locale of largely meaningless work and poignantly futile gestures of independence, with life outside the plant almost forced to become the locale of genuine self-expression and yet, despite relatively high pay, insufficiently dramatized by annual increments of durable consumer goods. He sees these increments— the new car, the better TV set, the barbecut pit—as more or less dictated by the mass media, by advertising; he cannot believe that these products and their care and feeding suffice for a good life or make up for the surrender of enthusiasm for or aspirations about work itself. Some critics may dismiss his misgivings as the biased judgment of an intellectual, imposing his standards on others; but I believe that his values are constructively used in the research, for they lead him to probe the consciousness of his respondents for signs of disaffection, and to see such signs in the recurrent dream of leaving the factory for a farm or small business. That is, he regards this dream of release as not merely a vestigial response to the success ethic but also as evidence that the life-style bought by factory monotony is, in profound respects, unsatisfying.

Such interpretations, of course, bring age-old controversies to bear on new material, and an introduction is no place for their resolution. Nor have I felt it incumbent on me, as I would in a review, to examine details of the book critically (though I should perhaps point out that for my taste, since I prefer density to ease of reading, the book is more painstakingly explanatory than it needs to be). Rather, my purpose is to show what is in the pudding by selecting a few raisins in the way of fact and of implication.

Let us travel with Chinoy, then, to "Autotown," a city of 100,000 or so which grew up with the industry. There he worked for a spell on the assembly line in a large plant, whose workers were to be the microcosm for further investigation. Introduced as a "worker," he turned into a "professor" and proceeded to do 78 long and searching interviews with 62 workers, men of varying seniority, most of them over thirty. The heart of the book is the analysis of these 62 studies in the light of Chinoy's questions about the American dream; these interviews in turn suggest, as we shall see, some ideas for further testing. They raise, for instance, the question whether the American dream of success has actually had much impact on these factory workers, and if so, at what stage of the life-cycle. Conceivably, those born in the lower class were early able to shut it out despite its pervasiveness in print and in some media, in much the same way that (as public opinion polls show) a large proportion of the electorate always manages to miss even the headline news, the names of its senators, and other facts which "everyone" knows. Likewise, it is arguable that Americans, especially in the lower strata, are not entirely immune to what might be termed the "dream of failure," the sometimes comforting fatalism of "you can't win" which can even undercut evidence of actual success, let alone the imperative that one ought to get ahead.

Chinoy also shows (what the non-specialist reader might take too readily for granted) that it is possible to get at workers' aspirations directly, by asking them, if one is sensitive and tactful. Chinoy had to pay a price, as every good interviewer does: he had to evade an interviewee's attempt to convert him to an evangelical sect, and had to listen to much else that was not relevant for him; interviewing in homes, he faced the usual problem of kibitzers (though he worked before the time when the competition of the TV set became a major hazard); he did not pay his informants, and had to hold their interest on occasion for as long as four hours. However, Chinoy did not overvalue his evocative interviews, all-purpose tool though they were, for he also gathered statistical data about the plant, and talked with management and with union officials concerning workers' aspirations and opportunities. Thus, he gained a context for questioning and for interpreting what he was told. If he did not approach the respondents as a worker, he at least was not an innocent surveyor.

That context is a plant with a wide range of jobs, much wider than the constricted range of pay. As we shall see, these jobs are differentially ranked in terms of their relative amenity, ease, and freedom of movement; thus, the assembly line, which enlists only a small proportion of auto workers, is regarded as undesirable, a cut or so above floor-sweeping or similar menial tasks. (The long-term trend towards the elimination of unskilled and "menial" jobs is evident in his figures, but not the effort of some of the auto companies, as indicated in Peter Drucker's *The Concept of the Corporation*, to eliminate the assembly line itself.) Promotions from job to job depend on seniority, with the result of limiting both "merit" and adventitious advances by individuals; Chinoy agrees with F. H. Harbison that the union is generally successful in enforcing the seniority rule. Thus, most men, if they stay with the "A.B.C." Company, can move in time to jobs of greater desirability and a bit more pay. A very few can become foreman, although many definitely do not want this "non-com" job, which carries so many more anxieties and isolations in return for a small increment of salary and status. And the foreman job is today the ceiling. Indeed, in the interviews no one had any goal in the plant above the first level of supervision, although in the executive group, as management unfailingly reminded itself and its help, were "holdovers" who had risen from the floor. If these models had once exercised a gravitational pull, it could not be measured by Chinoy's time.*

Recent work at Harvard and elsewhere has shown that, for most boys, the final decision about the white-collar and professional world is made in high school or earlier. Even bright youngsters, whose fathers are factory workers and who could afford to finish high school and go to college, frequently choose the immediate gratifications of a job, a car, a girl, and spending money—gratifications which for their fathers (whom they are taking as models) are already often becoming stale and unsatisfying. Yet if such a father tells his son that he wants him to go to college, he is saying, "Don't be like me," and the more the boy idealizes his father the harder it may be for him to accept this.†

Chinoy was fully aware of the fact that his interviews with workers were not elucidating the time of final decision concerning social mobility, but rather the time when all hope for promotion, or interest in it, is wholly abandoned. The age of thirty-five would seem to be the point of no return here. After that dreams of glory must be located not only outside the Company but also outside of much practical effort to make them come true. Thus, he was led to undertake a questionnaire study of the job aspirations of all boys graduating from Autotown's high schools in 1947 and 1948, by which time, of course, a good deal of sifting had already occurred. He found that 40 per cent of boys from working-class homes merely intended to "look for a job," nature unspecified, while another 20 per cent

---

* One possible exception was a college-trained timekeeper who hoped through a correspondence course in accounting to enter the accounting department; in general, it would seem to me, adult education courses, and much buying of books like those of Dale Carnegie, thrive on just such near-forlorn hopes—five years later, this man was still a timekeeper.

† Cf. Joseph A. Kahl, "Educational and Occupational Aspirations of 'Common Man' Boys," *Harvard Educational Review*, **23**:186–203 (1953).

either had some definite manual job in mind or were leaving the future to Uncle Sam. Asked whether he would give up "fun" to take a job which might promise future advancement, one eighteen-year-old senior said: "Do you want me to tell you the truth? I'd rather have fun." A dozen years later, with fun's limits tested, he may feel as did a machine operator who told Chinoy: "Sometimes I say to myself . . . you could have been somebody . . . if you hadn't been so interested in the almighty dollar [pursued, the context makes clear, not for its own sake but for the pleasures it bought]."

Chinoy suggests, in effect, that this working class, though native, behaves like other urban immigrants: it becomes acculturated to American values at their most shallow and short-run, victimized by the growing prestige of consumer goods and unable to escape the temptation of earning, after a very short spell of training (very far from a true apprenticeship), as much at twenty as their fathers do at forty or fifty.*

Chinoy's finding, that four of the six men who had definite hopes of becoming foremen had already advanced substantially within the job hierarchy in the plant, does not contradict but rather confirms the foregoing. For it shows how short and immediate is the timetable by which aspirations are controlled: only if at first you do succeed, will you try again. This persistence only when the pay-off is quick has been shown experimentally by psychologists who assign tasks to their subjects and find standards of performance to depend on early achievement. It is also shown historically by those revolutions which have been made, not by the chronically oppressed, but by strata which are rising quickly, though not quite fast enough.

Even so, those who appeared to have given up hope of advance still showed by their rationalizations that they were not wholly unsusceptible to the older moralities of upward and onward. These rationalizations took the form of making a mystery of promotion, of insisting that one couldn't tell what combination of effort and hard work, obsequiousness, and favoritism brought advance. Doing a good line job was often a way to assure being left there. Yet in a plant so well scheduled one did not attribute promotions to foreman ranks to luck. Very likely, the "GI" sort of abuse heaped on a worker who appeared to want the management's notice, who ingratiated himself with foremen, served partly to confirm the worker

---

* Chinoy's questionnaire shows that 23 per cent of the boys from middle-class homes also had short-run and vague career aims. It would be interesting to investigate this minority further—to see, for example, if some of these youngsters had been influenced by the view, now very common in the educated strata, that postponement of pleasure is inhibited and neurotic, and that working-class youth, with their many "outlets," are closer to "nature."

ideology that advance was hopeless, or could only be attained by loss of self- and group-respect—an ideology which made one's own lack of drive easier to bear while at the same time reinforcing it.

If vertical mobility is uncommon, sideways movement is common—most often, to get away from the assembly line with its overriding rhythm and watchful supervision. Some sought to satisfy idiosyncracies, like the desire to work alone, or outside, or on a big, new machine; most workers simply wanted an easy job, hard to supervise: not because they were lazy—they worked at home on their gardens and cars—but because the drama of work itself had gone stale for them by the time they had been in the plant a year or two. Judging from the quotations from interviews Chinoy gives, there is as I have already implied much talk in the plant about which are the desirable jobs, and gradations which seem small to the outsider loom large to the workers. Since it takes time to get in on such talk and so to be kept informed of openings, legal seniority is reinforced by the communications pattern. "Clean" work is an important desideratum: inspection and like jobs are sought after because they do not get one's hands greasy; and of course increasing automatization eliminates more and more of what is thought to be dirty work and thus perhaps still further derogates it.

Chinoy found no gross social and economic or age differences between those who had managed to find relative satisfaction in their jobs and those who bitterly resented them, nor did he have the opportunity (à la Hawthorne) to explore the differences of personality and personal life. Max Scheler's concept of *l'homme de ressentiment* might prove fruitful in further investigation, and several recent studies suggest that those most happy in a routine job are those for whom it matters least.

Nearly four fifths of the men interviewed had at some time contemplated leaving the factory. The great majority had an eye on small businesses; others wanted to be farmers; still others hoped to be salesmen, policemen, or other white-collar employees. Even those who liked their jobs, considering them "the best in the shop," had cherished a private dream of leaving the factory for good. The dream was not of a fortune, but of independence and old-age security.* Chinoy quotes a machine operator, more articulate than most, but typical in feeling, as follows:

"The main thing is to be independent and give your own orders and not have to take them from anybody else. That's the reason the fellows in the

---

* Chinoy observes that the workers know that oldsters are no longer simply fired, as they once were, but are shifted to unprestigeful jobs like sweeper or elevator man. He feels that these men cast their shadows before, and make the plant itself seem a graveyard for hope and energy.

shop all want to start their own business. Then the profits are all for yourself. When you're in the shop there's nothing in it for yourself. When
you put in a screw or a head on a motor, there's nothing for yourself in it.
So you just do what you have to in order to get along. A fellow would
rather do it for himself. If you expend the energy, it's for your own benefit
then."

If we put this quotation together with the search for cushy jobs within
the plant, we can see that one thing of which most wage workers are de-
prived is any chance to extend themselves, to go all-out, save in the ulti-
mately self-defeating ingenuity of quota-restriction. The colleague group,
plus one's own fear of being a sucker, effectively deprive one—as does the
rationalization imposed by time-study and division of labor—of much
variety of pace; the small businessman and farmer are free of direct colleagues and can go all-out (that this is also their peril is perhaps not fully
grasped by the factory workers). Walker and Guest's *The Man on the
Assembly Line*, which Chinoy cites with justified approbation, is further
testimony to the felt monotony both of work and non-work in the factory.
Indeed, the Walker-Guest study, done in New Haven, is quite consistent
with the Chinoy findings in midwestern Autotown. Reading these studies,
one wonders whether another war would not come as a relief to many of
these workers, allowing them to rise to a challenge and test their powers
against something stronger than a frightened foreman.

Of the 32 men who had dreams of small businesses, however, only eight
had done anything about them, while another nine had some sort of active
plans. Five years later, only three of this group had actually made it, and
all these had been men in their twenties, without much seniority. Those
wanting to become farmers were up against the fact that farming requires
increasing amounts of capital, a commodity rendered scarcer by the
workers' tendency, already indicated, to buy homes and expensive consumer goods which in effect tie them to the city. Those who dreamed of
their own businesses would not need much money. They dreamed of
garages and groceries, of a bake shop and a tool-and-die shop or of starting
a tourist place up north where one could rent out cabins and boats and sell
supplies to hunters and fishermen, thus combining one's work with a
favorite Autotown vacation. The men in the shop all knew of people who
had followed such routes to advancement. Thousands of small businesses
had sprung up in and around Autotown after the war. But they also knew
of those who had failed (the mortality rate in small business has always
been high) and had come back to the supervision and security of the plant.
Indeed, of Chinoy's respondents seven had once had small businesses, and

another seven, farms.* "I've got a family and I can't take chances"—this was the refrain Chinoy heard over and over from those who had relinquished active plans for leaving, while not entirely surrendering the dream.

By this stage, the dream has become little more than the substratum for griping; and perhaps it enters as a counter into the general pressure for wage boosts and fringe benefits, although every raise and every increment of security, as Chinoy shows, makes it that much harder to think of leaving the plant. Moreover, at least up to a point, talk about one's plans to leave brings prestige in the shop—though this may boomerang if the talker does not eventually act.†

Chinoy's chapter on "The Chronology of Aspirations" indicates that the point of no return is rather rapidly passed for the auto worker. By the time he is in his late thirties, he has too much seniority, too much familiarity, too much family, to be willing to pull up stakes. In his study of York, England, before World War I, B. Seebohm Rowntree concluded that the career of the urban worker could be described as a "poverty cycle" in which, for only a brief period of early adulthood, one could live on a plateau slightly elevated above subsistence, before one's accumulating progeny and weakening strength brought one down to the Plimsoll line of grinding and bare existence. For the workers of Autotown, the $50-$60 a

---

* Careful studies of labor mobility in the Oakland, California, area by S. M. Lipset and Reinhard Bendix show rather high amounts of movement both ways between factory work and small entrepreneurship. This is entirely compatible with Chinoy's observation that small business rather than promotion is seen in Autotown as the main alternative to factory work. Still, there are probably regional differences, as well as differences among industries. Steelworkers in Gary, according to Warner Bloomberg, Jr., not infrequently hold two jobs at once, of which one may be in a small business such as a filling station: the second job may sop up energies not demanded in the modern mill and also provide a sort of trial balloon for an entire break from the mill. Other studies also show the two-job pattern spreading, as factory hours become shorter and less tiring, while at the same time the "standard of living" demands for the All-American Family rise. (I suppose that workers in some of the auto plants who spend time on the job selling policy slips can be said to hold two jobs, but Chinoy did not turn up any of these.)

† Fred H. Blum's book, based on a study of the Hormel packing plant in Austin, Minnesota, suggests that a lack of emotional identification with the union may be one result of the retention of such dreams—while at the same time the long life of the dream depends on the use of the union as an insurance premium. He writes of "the case of an elderly worker who would really like to be independent. An emotional identification with the union is impossible for him without acknowledging that the desire to be his own boss is merely a dream. . . . By leaving his feelings towards the union sufficiently cool, his dream of independence can glow affectionately. On the other hand, he is elderly and he knows that his job would be endangered without seniority. He appreciates, therefore, the services rendered by the union: 'being able to meet with the company *as a group* and talk over *our* troubles and seniority.' " *Toward a Democratic Work Process* (N.Y.: Harper & Bro., 1953), p. 43 (italics mine).

week plateau is ever so much higher; there are some reserves; there are pension rights; yet for that great majority who do not escape the plant, Chinoy's interviews show work to be regarded as a form of daily part-time imprisonment, through which one pays off the fines incurred by one's pursuit of the good, or rather the "good time," life at home and on vacations. It is hard, of course, to know to what extent feelings of general dissatisfaction with life, or with one's wife, are displaced onto the factory (as Mayo, and Roethlisberger and Dixon noted in their Western Electric studies), or vice versa. Existence is at times a prison for virtually all of us, and we express our desire for escape in dreams, hymns, the movies, and in many other ways. The notion that a man should not dislike his work is basic to Chinoy's book and those of Blum and many other industrial sociologists; yet given the not wholly unfortunate lack of congruence between human beings and their work, there is something to be said for escapism. Paradoxically, escapism militates against self-deception as to whether one *does* like one's work, in the face of the efforts of the management to foster guilt in those whose morale, apart from their performance, is Cassius-like and low.

For the older workers, the union itself offers something of a second chance (that second chance which is so large a constituent of dreams) for a career with some entrepreneurial aspects. Many locals, I suppose, can be compared to small businesses which are parts of a larger chain. But none of the routes which workers take or even dream about offer the big money, but merely the chance to rise above what we can no longer term the "poverty cycle" but what we might better term the "standard of living" or the "necessary luxury" cycle.

Many of these matters are highlighted by an interview Chinoy reports with a 22-year-old single man, who was very proud of having managed, by threatening to quit, to get transferred from the assembly line to the job of driving completed cars off the end of the line. New cars, along with baseball and girls, meant much to him. He had recently bought a new A.B.C. car, but was planning to replace it when next year's model came out, and one of his reasons for working at A.B.C. was the large discount on new cars given to employees. He told Chinoy, "I don't intend to stay here forever," but in view of his lack of concrete plans for work, as against his very concrete plans for play, and making play of his work, this was an idle boast. If we recall what horses have meant to knights, or to Arabs, we might modify somewhat Chinoy's judgment that cars cannot be a way of life for long; in any case, Chinoy realizes that he would have to re-interview this "chauffeur" in a later phase of the cycle, and that this longitudinal study is not quite encompassed by interviews with workers who are now older and still in the plant. Much will depend on what happens to his friends, and

on the particular breaks of shift and supervision. In fact, even within the
space of a few months a number of Chinoy's respondents vacillated in
their attitudes towards factory work, depending on whether they were
working days or nights, whether they had a good guy for a foreman, or
similar happenstance.

While most of us in the middle class can be said to have a career only
retroactively, we certainly can look back on more moves, up and sideways,
and hence look forward also to more, from the base of a more complex
personal history. While the executive life may be becoming increasingly
security-minded, it has not come anywhere near reaching the semantics by
which, as Chinoy reveals, the Autotown workers equate security with getting ahead, as in the following remark by a truck driver with three children:

> "If you've got security, if you've got something you can fall back on,
> you're still getting ahead";

or, to the same effect, "If you work during a layoff . . . that's my idea of
working up." No less revealing is the remark of a welder:

> "I don't think a person should be satisfied. My next step is a nice little
> modern house of my own. That's what I mean by bettering yourself—or
> getting ahead."

Here, as Chinoy points out, "the backward art of spending money" has become the forward salient of the life-cycle.

Modern social research cannot do without such fieldworkers as Chinoy.
They are the descendants of the turn-of-the-century explorers who brought
us the news about how the "other half" lives once we could no longer
assume, with the arrogance of a homogeneous people, that their lives were
like ours, only less comfortable. All sorts of questions of course remain:
whether other factory workers are like auto-workers; whether life is different in Detroit; whether women, who have fewer hopes to start with and
far less pressure for achievement, may not find factory work more liber-
ating than men do; and what will happen to the worker when he has his
"nice little modern home"—we must ask as psychologists as well as economists whether the domestic package is infinitely expansible. But whatever
industry may mean to the worker, it remains an expansible frontier for the
researcher; and his factory adventure on which Chinoy reports serves in
topic and treatment as a model for further advance.

DAVID RIESMAN

I

Tradition and Reality

This book reports an investigation of what opportunity looks and feels like to a group of automobile workers in a middle-sized midwestern city. It is an attempt to explore how these men live out their versions of the American dream in a world in which there is a palpable disparity between their experience and the prevalent myth.

The United States has been widely pictured as a "land of promise" where golden opportunities beckon to able and ambitious men without regard to their original station in life. The Horatio Alger sagas of "little tykes who grow into big tycoons," it is asserted, "truly express a commonplace of American experience."[1] School children learn early of humble Americans whose careers fulfilled the promise, and occasional new arrivals at the top of the success ladder are publicly acclaimed as fresh illustrations that opportunity is always open to those who "have what it takes." The American Schools and Colleges Association, for example, annually presents "Horatio Alger Awards" with much fanfare to businessmen whose "rise to success symbolizes the tradition of starting from scratch under our system of free competitive enterprise."[2]

Based upon some concrete facts plus a substantial admixture of mythology* and optimism, this tradition of opportunity and success has long been a folk gospel deeply imbedded in American life. The phenomenal circulation of the classics of the opportunity-success literature—perhaps twenty million copies of Horatio Alger's stories, forty million copies of Elbert Hubbard's *Message to Garcia*, the public delivery by Russell H. Conwell of his famous lecture *Acres of Diamonds* to an estimated six thousand audiences—testifies to its wide acceptance in the past. Although there are few recent contributions popular enough to match these now-obsolete classics (books by Horatio Alger have become prized items among biblio-

---

* "Poor immigrant boys and poor farm boys who became business leaders have always been more conspicuous in American history books than in the American business elite." W. Miller: "American Historians and the American Business Elite," *Journal of Economic History* 9:184–200 (November, 1949).

philes), the still substantial volume of contemporary "how to be successful" literature indicates the persisting vitality of the tradition. Perhaps the closest equivalent to a modern classic in this field is Dale Carnegie's *How to Win Friends and Influence People*. But there is also an imposing array of books and magazines which, supplemented by an unceasing flow of newspaper material and public speeches, affirms the reality of opportunity and the possibility of success, and suggests the prerequisites required, the avenues to be followed, and the techniques to be used.

The pervasive American dream, however, has on occasion also been consciously and deliberately stimulated for political and ideological reasons. The idea that "the wheel of fortune is in constant operation and the poor in one generation furnish the rich in the next," enunciated by Edward Everett in 1839 as part of the ideological counterattack against class-conscious Jacksonian democracy,[3] is still being used in an effort to insulate existing institutions against change. In conjunction with large corporations which were rendered defensive by the events of the post-1929 decades, the media of mass communication have tried to bolster the big-business version of free enterprise by energetically fostering the belief that, to quote one newspaper advertisement: "The young men and women of today have before them opportunities far greater than have existed since the beginning of time."[4]

The American experience has indeed been distinctive in the opportunities it has offered. The expansion across a rich unpeopled continent of a population that roughly doubled every twenty-five years from 1790 to 1914 enabled farm boys, bookkeepers, peddlers, clerks and mechanics to rise in the world, to become in some cases captains of industry and titans of finance. From the ranks of millions of immigrants came a few who climbed to wealth and prominence, while in an expanding economy each wave of new arrivals pushed upward the children of those who had come earlier.

But the events of recent decades—the cessation of mass immigration, the leveling of the rate of population increase, the growth of giant corporations with specialized technical and managerial staffs, and the concentration of industry—have seemed to some students to be choking off opportunities for individual advancement. One authority, for example, has asserted that "The long-existing favorable balance of vertical circulation of individuals in American society, i.e., the excess of upward over downward moves, has diminished and seems likely to be further reduced."[5]

Others, while recognizing the fact that the character of opportunity has changed, have denied that there is less vertical mobility than in the past. They have pointed to basic occupational and economic trends which may counterbalance any forces slowing down the rate of upward mobility. These trends include the shift of employment from production to service and distributive industries, the steady increase in the proportion of white-collar and professional workers, the opening of new fields such as popular entertainment and professional sports, the emergence of a new type of entrepreneur—the public relations adviser, the five-percenter, the lobbyist—who moves in the interstices between imperfectly integrated bureaucratic organizations or who represents these organizations to the public.[6]

There has also been increasing evidence that Americans have tended to interpret the past more in terms of folklore than of facts, that opportunities for vertical mobility were never as great as generally assumed and therefore could not have declined very much. William Miller has shown, for example, that the Horatio Alger sagas had little relationship to the careers of those who were the American business elite in 1900, that is, those who began their careers about 1870.[7] The "safety-valve theory" which saw the frontier as an outlet for ambitious and dissatisfied urban workers has been shown to have little historical validity.[8] The steadily increasing dominance of big business has tended to obscure the fact that the proportion of independent businessmen has remained relatively constant for the past sixty years and that the rate of failure among entrepreneurs has probably always been very high.[9] What has appeared to some as a decline in opportunity may be merely a progressive awakening from an illusion created by the nation's extraordinary economic growth.

A definitive conclusion as to whether there has actually been a decline in the rate of social mobility in American society must necessarily wait upon further research, upon studies of the recruitment and careers, both past and present, not only of business leaders, but also of professionals, successful small businessmen, corporate managers at all levels, and of those who have achieved success in the newer occupational fields.

Whatever the historical trends, it is abundantly clear that factory workers, with whom we are concerned in this study, are severely handicapped in their pursuit of economic advancement. In this era of big business, with its demands for specialized managerial and technical skills and its high capital requirements for successful entrepreneurial ventures, the factory workers' plight in seeking to rise in the world might be likened to that of the traveler whose query about the route to his destination elicited from a pragmatic farmer the reply: "If I were you I wouldn't start from here in the first place." "It is widely recognized," declared the authors of a report prepared for the Temporary National Economic Committee in 1940, "that substantial opportunity does not exist for a large proportion of workers in either small or large corporations. . . . Most of them, therefore, must look forward to remaining more or less at the same levels, despite the havoc this might visit upon the tradition of 'getting ahead.' "[10]

Industrial workers, therefore, are caught between the promises of a widely affirmed tradition and the realities of the contemporary economic and social order. The nature of this conflict between tradition and reality in which they find themselves becomes clearly evident when we examine the paths to the top which are recommended to the hopeful and ambitious.

Tradition strongly sanctions independent business enterprise as a realistic way for the "little man" to achieve economic success without reference to the problems that confront an aspiring entrepreneur in a world of monopoly and big business. This small-business tradition found classic expression in Abraham Lincoln's oft-repeated* statement to Congress in 1861:

> . . . there is not of necessity any such thing as the free hired laborer being fixed to that condition for life. . . . The prudent, penniless beginner in the world, labors for wages awhile, saves a surplus with which to buy tools or land for himself, then labors on his own account for awhile, and at length hires another new beginner to help him. This is the just, and generous, and prosperous system; which opens the way to all—gives hope to all, and consequent energy and progress, and improvement of conditions to all.[11]

Small business remains a continually stimulated ambition, concretized in frequent newspaper stories and advertisements. "They Fulfilled the G.I. Dream: 'A Business of My Own' " reads one newspaper headline typical of numerous others. Even the weekly paper published by the C.I.O. unions in the city where this study was undertaken frequently carried accounts of automobile workers who had ventured into small business. If there are no immediately visible instances of business success in one's home town, there are always examples of the "rags to riches saga" in business which are brought close by radio, movies, magazines, or newspapers. *Life*, for example, in presenting an account of the growth of an automobile dealer's business in Kankakee, Illinois, as a "U.S. Success Story" commented:

> But Romy [the businessman] was no isolated example. In other Kankakees were other Romy's. . . . In America the dream was still there for those who believed it strongly enough to roll up their sleeves.[12]

"All men are free," declared a full-page advertisement defending business profits which appeared in the New York *Herald Tribune*, "to work where they please, invest hard-earned dollars, plow earnings back, grow, expand, progress—and never stop."[13]

For men on the level of wage labor, this "freedom" is severely cramped

---

* See, for example, the use made of this statement in "Your Chance of Getting Ahead," an editorial in *Business Week*, June 7, 1947, p. 80. This editorial was simultaneously published as an advertisement in various newspapers.

by the facts of business life. Although it is fairly easy to go into business—an average of about 400,000 new businesses have been started annually in recent years—the odds against success are high, particularly for those with little capital. It has been estimated that usually thirty per cent of new businesses do not survive their first year and an additional fourteen per cent do not live through the second, although the figures vary widely from industry to industry.[14] Concentration of much of the nation's business in the hands of relatively few large corporations has left chiefly the more hazardous, less profitable lines to new enterprisers seeking to realize the American dream. And "newcomers with limited capital resources are confined to those trades where profits are lowest and failure rates high—trades where entrance is easy, competition high, and consequently survival chances poor."[15] Men are still free to try their hands at an independent business venture, if they can raise some capital, but as one student of small business has pointed out: "Freedom to enter a trade only to fail and dissipate resources is the freedom of a captured crew to 'walk the plank.' "[16]

If savings are inadequate to start a business or the risks seem too great, men may seek to follow the alternative route recommended by tradition, ascent through a corporate hierarchy. The sharp increase in the number and proportions of administrative, clerical and technical positions in industry that accompanied the growth of giant corporations* undoubtedly created desirable new positions for men rising from the ranks. Indeed, C. Wright Mills has suggested that small business as the route to success is being supplanted by a "new way up," the "white collar way: to get a job within a government or business hierarchy and to rise according to the rules that prevail from one prearranged step to another."[17] The path to success within industry is frequently and emphatically described as open to the lowliest factory employee. That the ladder to the top starts from one's job, wherever it may be in the corporate hierarchy, is a recurrent theme. For example, Alfred P. Sloan, Chairman of the Board of General Motors, recommends in his autobiography, titled perhaps suggestively *Adventures of a White Collar Man:*

> Think of the corporation as a pyramid of opportunities from the bottom toward the top with thousands of chances for advancement. Only capacity limited any worker's chances to grow, to develop his ability to make a greater contribution to the whole and to improve his own position as well. The routes to the heights in industry were open to all, even though in-

---

* From 1899 to 1947 the ratio of administrative, clerical, and technical employees to production workers in industry rose from 9.9 to 22. This increase probably exaggerates the increase in opportunity to some extent, however, since many of these new positions were undoubtedly dead-end clerical and secretarial jobs for women. S. Melman: "The Rise of Administrative Overhead in the Manufacturing Industries of the United States," *Oxford Economic Papers* (New Series) 3:89 (February, 1951).

creasingly and inexorably the big chances beckoned to those with unusual qualifications and trained minds. The Fisher brothers had climbed; Knudsen had climbed. And in the General Motors Corporation thousands of others had climbed to some degree of eminence in the structure.[18]

But as Mr. Sloan points out, the qualifications for advancement in industry are now very demanding. The organizational complexity and the extensive mechanization of industry make university education or some form of technical training a major prerequisite for the positions with the greatest promise and the best pay. For men without special training or advanced education who go to work on the factory floor there are sharp limits on the possibility of future advancement.[19] Two ladders of advancement seem to have emerged in industry. One, open to workers, is short, with few rungs, usually ending with foremanship. The other, open to those whose education and training enable them to begin as technicians or white-collar workers, is longer, and may eventually lead to the top levels of industry.[20] The occupational fate of men in industry, therefore, is virtually determined when they end their education. Working-class youth, even if they possess the capacity for further education, are likely to cease their formal training before they can acquire the knowledge and skills which might increase their chances of getting ahead.* In the words of the President's Commission on Higher Education, "The old comfortable idea that 'any boy can get a college education who has it in him' simply is not true."[21]

These limitations on the industrial worker's chances to get on in the world either as an entrepreneur or within some corporate hierarchy are sharply discounted by the staunchly individualistic bias of the tradition. "Your future is strictly up to you," begins a pamphlet prepared by the National Association of Manufacturers for distribution to youth.[22] Obstacles such as poverty or lack of education will inevitably be overcome by those who "have what it takes," by those who do not give up their ambition or cease their efforts, come what may. Indeed, poverty itself is sometimes defined as a useful spur to ambition and effort. "Hardship did not stir me to revolt," declared Eric Johnston, "it only served as a spur to my ambition."[23] Objective features in success are ignored in the calendar of prerequisites for economic achievement; the advantages of inherited wealth and family position, for example, are rarely mentioned as reasons why some men occupy high places.

In its definition of how to get ahead, as well as in its description of the opportunities presumably open to everyone, tradition does not square with

* For an analysis of this problem in relation to the aspirations of working-class youth, see Chapter IX.

reality. Taken as a whole, the prescriptions for success are vague and un-reliable. They define patterns of behavior which are supposed to be useful in getting on in the world and offer recipes for self-development without regard to the different abilities and skills needed to succeed in various fields —in the factory, in a small grocery, in a radio-repair shop or gasoline station, for example—and the opportunities available to men engaged in factory labor either to acquire or display the capacities required for success.

The ambiguity and uncertainty of the prescriptions for success are most clearly evident in the stress upon the "economic potency of character."[24] "Your opportunities will be limited only by your vision of what your future may become, your abilities and how you use them, your character and your determination," proclaimed the N.A.M. pamphlet quoted above.[25] The time-honored journalistic question: "To what do you owe your success?" elicits from prominent citizens a heterogeneous array of personal qualities which are then recommended to the ambitious as "keys to success." In 1947 when B. C. Forbes asked the men whom he listed as "America's Fifty Foremost Business Leaders" to what they owed their preeminence, their answers included enthusiasm, confidence, simplicity, frankness, energy, courage, foresight, physical fitness, judgment, imagination, determination, self-control, and tolerance.[26] Precisely how to go about acquiring, utilizing, or demonstrating these traits is nowhere indicated.

In this age of salesmanship and bureaucracy, however, character as the basis for success has, in a sense, been externalized.* The traditional pre-requisites for getting on in the world—perseverance, determination, am-bition, resourcefulness—were *in* the individual; the newer prescriptions deal with externals, with those things which impress others. As C. W. Mills has pointed out: "The success literature has shifted with the success pattern. It is still focussed upon personal virtues, but they are not the sober virtues once imputed to successful entrepreneurs. Now the stress is on agility rather than ability, on 'getting along' in a context of associates, superiors, and rules, rather than 'getting ahead' across an open market; on who you know rather than what you know; on techniques of self-display and the generalized knack of handling people rather than on moral integrity, substantive accom-plishments, and solidity of person."[27] An enormous mass of popular litera-ture suggests how to mold oneself into the "successful personality." The tremendous circulation of Dale Carnegie's *How to Win Friends and In-fluence People* testifies not only to the prevalent loneliness of urban Ameri-

---

* For a penetrating discussion of some aspects of this change, see D. Riesman: *The Lonely Crowd*, New Haven, Yale University Press, 1950. Riesman goes further, however, to suggest that the stress upon personality leads to a change in the meaning of success, with the approval of one's peers becoming more important than objective economic achievement. See pp. 144–147.

cans, but also to the contemporary stress upon the manipulation of personality as a means to success.*

However important the personality attributes which facilitate social intercourse may be to those who work with people, they can have only limited significance to those who work with things. In order to leave the factory or gain entry to the managerial hierarchy, men must usually have considerably more than personality to offer. It is only after they leave the factory or move into management that they can find much value in these new prescriptions.

The shift from character to personality, however, has not changed the status of the traditional imperative of unremitting industry and effort. One must be willing to work hard, to put in long hours, to do whatever has to be done, no matter how difficult it may be. Hard work, one is frequently reminded, is the essential ingredient in every successful career; those whose efforts do not slacken will eventually be rewarded. As with all other aspects of the tradition, and perhaps even more so, an endless array of illustrations is available from which one can only arbitrarily select. For example, a recent inspirational book for youth consisting of biographies of business leaders found the secret of their success in the slogan, "Let your work be your life."[28] The startling success of Charles Nash, who began as a dollar-a-day hand in an automobile plant and eventually headed General Motors and then his own company, was attributed by a newspaper writer to his "capacity for work."[29] But as our earlier discussion indicates, the industrious factory worker without other qualifications has little chance of rising in industry or of being able to embark upon a small business venture. And, as we shall see later, hard work can have little value as a means of impressing one's boss or of increasing one's income in a mass-production industry with its carefully timed jobs.

Nor have the newer formulas for success displaced the familiar slogan, "Build a better mousetrap and the world will beat a path to your door," a prescription of particular relevance to men who work with their hands. Despite the changes which have occurred in the character of technological innovation, the inventiveness of a Thomas A. Edison or an Alexander Graham Bell is still held up as a sure means of becoming rich. "Makes a Better Clothesline so Housewives Beat a Path" read one newspaper headline.† Such encouragement may inspire hope among men with mechanical

* Research should be directed to the psychological consequences of this instrumental utilization of the self in which one judges one's personality in terms of its success in meeting the standards of others and of the marketability of one's personal traits. See E. Fromm: *Man for Himself*, New York, Rinehart and Company, Inc., 1947, pp. 67–82.

† In this merchandising age, however, the slogan is sometimes qualified by reference to the necessity to floodlight the path to one's door by advertising, a prerequisite that places more obstacles in the path of the ingenious inventor.

ingenuity, but it takes no account of the fact that new-product development and new-machine design are now very largely the result of sustained scientific research conducted primarily by giant corporations. According to one study, "Groups of specialists working in large, industrial laboratories, owned by vast corporate organizations, are replacing the isolated inventor."[30] Because of the gap between worker and technician, the ingenious mechanic in industry is more likely to receive only an occasional bonus for his suggestions than recognition of his abilities by steady occupational advancement.

By thus finding the "secret of success" in what the individual is and does, the tradition of opportunity not only distracts attention from large institutional obstacles, it also encourages men who lack influence, money, or education. Even without these advantages men may hope to gain advancement by working hard, by showing mechanical ingenuity, or by cultivating an attractive personality. They may persist in their efforts sustained by the belief that perseverance, ambition, and determination must eventually earn their just reward.

Maintenance of a high level of aspiration which is thus encouraged by the assurance that there are rich opportunities and that success eventually comes to the deserving is also required as evidence of full participation in American life. "Failure" is defined as withdrawal from the race as well as the inability to cross the finish line a winner. "Failure is ceasing to try! 'Tis admitting defeat," writes Edgar Guest. And to admit defeat is to confess one's inadequacies, for failure cannot be due to lack of opportunity, but can only result from lack of ambition or ability, from unwillingness to make the necessary sacrifices, or from defects in one's character and personality.

Industrial workers therefore face the following dilemma. On the one hand they are encouraged to aim high and to persist relentlessly; they are provided with an array of prescriptions for success; they are burdened with full responsibility for their fate. On the other hand they live in a world of only limited opportunity. The task of this book is to explore the problems created for workers by this disparity between tradition and reality and to examine what "opportunity" means to industrial workers, specifically to a group of automobile workers.

Footnotes to Chapter I

1. E. Johnston: *America Unlimited*, New York, Doubleday, Doran and Company, Inc., 1944, pp. 5–6.
2. Press Release, American Schools and Colleges Association, July 7, 1949.
3. Edward Everett: "Address Before the Mercantile Library Association, 1839," quoted in A. M. Schlesinger, Jr.: *The Age of Jackson*, New York, Little, Brown & Co., 1945, pp. 270–271.

4. Firestone Tire and Rubber Company advertisement, *The New York Times*, January 2, 1948, p. 47.

5. E. Sibley: "Some Demographic Clues to Stratification," *Amer. Sociol. Review* 7:322 (1942). See also J. O. Hertzler: "Some Tendencies Toward a Closed Class System in the United States," *Social Forces* 30:313–323 (March, 1952).

6. See C. W. Mills: "The Competitive Personality," *Partisan Review*, September-October, 1946, pp. 433–441.

7. W. Miller: "American Historians and the Business Elite," *J. Econ. History* 9:184–200 (November, 1949). See also his "The Recruitment of the Business Elite," *Quarterly J. Economics* 64:242–253 (May, 1950) and "The Business Elite in Business Bureaucracies," in W. Miller, Ed.: *Men in Business*, Cambridge, Harvard University Press, 1952, pp. 286–305.

8. See C. Goodrich and S. Davidson: "The Wage-Earner in the Western Movement," *Political Science Quarterly* 50:161–185 (June, 1935) and 51:61–116 (March, 1936); F. A. Shannon: "The Homestead Act and the Labor Surplus," *Amer. Historical Review* 41:637–651 (July, 1936) and "A Post-Mortem on the Labor-Safety-Valve Theory," *Agricultural History* 19:31–37 (January, 1945).

9. See K. Mayer: "Small Business as a Social Institution," *Social Research* 14:332–349 (September, 1947).

10. M. Dimock and H. K. Hyde: *Bureaucracy and Trusteeship in Large Corporations*, Temporary National Economic Committee Monographs, No. 11, Washington, D.C., Government Printing Office, 1940, p. 55.

11. From the Annual Message to Congress, December 3, 1861, from R. F. Basler, Ed.: *Abraham Lincoln, His Speeches and Writings*, Cleveland, The World Publishing Company, 1946, p. 634.

12. *Life*, September 23, 1946, p. 29.

13. Advertisement of the Standard Steel Spring Company, New York *Herald Tribune*, June 8, 1949.

14. These estimates are from Mayer, *op. cit.*, p. 337. See also A. R. Oxenfeldt, *New Firms and Free Enterprise*, Washington, D.C., American Council on Public Affairs, 1943, pp. 173–174.

15. Mayer, *op. cit.*, p. 338.

16. Oxenfeldt, *op. cit.*, p. 179.

17. Mills, *op. cit.*, p. 436.

18. A. P. Sloan, Jr.: *Adventures of a White Collar Man*, New York, Doubleday, Doran and Company, Inc., 1941, p. 153. Copyright by A. P. Sloan, Jr. and Boyden Sparks, reprinted by permission of Doubleday & Company, Inc.

19. For a precise description of how mechanization of the textile industry, for example, has narrowed the opportunities for workers to rise into management, see E. D. Smith: *Technology and Labor*, New Haven, Yale University Press, 1939, pp. 130–133.

20. See J. McConnell: *The Evolution of Social Classes*, Washington, D.C., American Council on Public Affairs, 1942, "Men in routine clerical jobs are at the beginning of their business careers; men in the wage earning category are set for life," pp. 87–88. See also R. S. and H. M. Lynd: *Middletown in Transition*, New York, Harcourt, Brace & Company, 1937, pp. 67–72.

21. *Higher Education for American Democracy: A Report of the President's Commission on Higher Education*, New York, Harper & Brothers, 1948, Volume I, *Establishing the Goals*, p. 28. For full documentation, see Volume II, *Equalizing and Expanding Individual Opportunity*, Chapters 2 and 3. One should, of course, note the wide regional differences in higher education as well as substantial differences in educational opportunity for rural and urban youth.

22. *Your Future Is What You Make It*, Fourth You and Industry Series, New York, National Association of Manufacturers, 1951, p. 3.

23. E. Johnston, *op. cit.*, p. 6.

24. This phrase is drawn from A. W. Griswold: "New Thought: A Cult of Success," *Amer. J. Sociol.* **40**:309–318 (November, 1934).
25. *Your Future Is What You Make It*, p. 3.
26. B. C. Forbes: *America's Fifty Foremost Business Leaders*, New York, B. C. Forbes Publishing Company, 1948, *passim*.
27. C. W. Mills: *White Collar*, New York, Oxford University Press, 1951, p. 263. Reprinted by permission of the publisher.
28. J. A. Moore: *Famous Leaders of Industry*, Fifth Series, Boston, L. C. Page, 1945, p. vi.
29. New York *Herald Tribune*, June 17, 1948.
30. L. L. Lorwin: *Technology in Our Economy*, Temporary National Economic Committee Monographs, No. 22, Washington, D.C., Government Printing Office, 1941, p. 208.

II

Automobiles and Opportunity

Automobile workers were chosen for this study because to a marked degree they face in their occupational lives the problems related to opportunity for industrial workers. Predominantly semiskilled, they work in a glamorous, relatively new industry whose growth has dramatized the American tradition of opportunity, but whose present character makes it extremely difficult for them to realize the American dream.

In 1951 the automobile industry ranked first among manufacturing industries in the number of production workers employed (660,810) and in the value added to its products by manufacturing ($5,912,525,000).[1] It was primarily the automobile industry's growth in the first decades of the century, however, that gave resounding new substance to the American success story. In those years the industry created new economic heroes, brought fabulous wealth to its owners and managers, and promised spectacular wages to men whose fathers had worked for a dollar a day. Table 1 indicates the speed and extent of that growth. In 1899 the industry, still in swaddling clothes, consisted of only fifty-seven establishments employing slightly over two thousand workers. Total output that year was just under four thousand cars. In 1919, 343,000 men were employed, and almost two million cars and trucks were produced.

Table 1

GROWTH OF THE AUTOMOBILE INDUSTRY, 1899–1919

Year	Production Workers (in ooo's)	Per Cent Increase	Automobiles Built* (in ooo's)	Per Cent Increase
1899	2	. .	4	. .
1904	12	600	23	475
1909	76	533	127	452
1914	127	67	573	351
1919	343	170	1,876	227

* Including trucks and busses.

Source: *Automobile Facts and Figures*, 28th Edition, Detroit, Automobile Manufacturers Association, 1948, pp. 4, 35.

The men who put the nation on wheels in those years were archetypal Horatio Alger heroes. Heading the list was Henry Ford, the farm boy and mechanic whose swift climb to worldwide fame and astonishing wealth provided a giant-size example of what could be done. As the man held responsible for the wonders of the assembly line, Ford became the symbol of the mass-production age which would bring abundance to the millions; as the sponsor of the "five-dollar day" he became the "benevolent hero of the capitalist saga"; as the "world's first billionaire" he was listened to with respect as he reiterated to an admiring public the very maxims which his ascent seemed to illustrate.[2] Ranged behind Ford in the automobile wing of the Horatio Alger pantheon were numerous others: William Knudsen, the Danish immigrant who earned a reputation as a production genius with Ford before moving to General Motors, which he eventually headed; Walter Chrysler, the railroad machinist who founded and directed one of the industry's Big Three; the Fisher brothers, skilled mechanics who became the automobile-body builders for General Motors before becoming part of the Corporation.

During the initial years of automobile manufacturing, economic advancement was possible both in independent enterprise and by ascent within a large organization. The ambitious enterprisers and the ingenious mechanics who envisioned the automobile's future found entry to the expanding industry fairly easy. Comparatively little capital was needed, since automobile production consisted chiefly of designing the car and assembling parts bought from others on short-term credit.* "The pioneers, for the most part young men, had large visions and little cash."[3] Between 1902 and 1908 seventy-seven companies successfully produced automobiles on a commercial scale.[4] But the number of enterprises that attempted to enter the market was much greater. In a 1916 study of automobile registration in Massachusetts, for example, 676 different makes of cars were reported.[5] Many of these enterprises were begun with stock issues to the participants that represented hope in the future rather than cash in the bank. The Ford Motor Company, the outstanding illustration, started business in 1903 with an initial capitalization, on paper, of $100,000, but with only $28,000 in its treasury.

Many of these ventures failed, but those which managed to survive earned staggering profits, paying their owners handsomely while simultane-

---

* "The chief business of the automobile producer, after the design of his product and the placing of orders for parts, was the assembling of the major components and the sale of the completed vehicle. The process of assembling was a short one; it required neither large plant nor elaborate equipment; and the land and buildings were as often rented as purchased." L. H. Seltzer: *A Financial History of the American Automobile Industry*, Boston, Houghton Mifflin Company, 1928, p. 20.

ously obeying the injunction to "plow earnings back, grow, progress—and never stop." So rich were profits in the industry that its extraordinary growth was financed almost completely out of earnings.[6] The Ford Motor Company, for example, earned almost $55,000,000 in its first ten years, and then over $100,000,000 in the next three years. Without issuing any stock to the public or floating any bond issues to finance its expansion, the company possessed, as of August 1, 1916, assets of $132,000,000, surplus of $112,000,-000, and cash and bonds worth $54,000,000.[7] In 1904, five years after the incorporation of the Olds Motor Works and only eleven years after he had driven his first car on the streets of Lansing, Ransom E. Olds, another of the early automobile magnates, retired as a millionaire. But his retirement was short-lived as home-town businessmen in Lansing hopefully offered him the capital with which to start the Reo Motor Car Company. This new venture, which began with $170,000 in cash and with property worth $130,-000, paid out over five million dollars in cash dividends in its first ten years and turned back more than four million dollars of profits into company expansion. Even some of the companies which expired after a few years managed to reap rich profits during their brief lives, while many of the men who saw automobile companies sink under them were able to start afresh or to secure executive positions with the survivors.[8]

In the burgeoning automobile plants, men who demonstrated mechanical ingenuity or administrative ability could see limitless possibilities. The practical mechanics and ambitious enterprisers who developed the industry chose many of their lieutenants from men who started on the factory floor in the early days of automobile production. Charles Nash at General Motors and Charles Sorenson at Ford were striking examples. It was with some justification, though not with total accuracy, that Henry Ford could write in 1922:

> All of our people have thus come up from the bottom. The head of the factory started as a machinist. Another man in charge of the big River Rouge plant began as a pattern maker. Another man overseeing one of the departments started as a sweeper. There is not a single man anywhere in the factory who did not simply come in off the street.[9]

At the same time inventors with useful suggestions could secure an attentive reception from automobile producers. The name of Charles Kettering stands out most clearly in this connection, but many others found their way to success in the industry by solving one or another of the innumerable problems that were faced in developing both the automobile and the technology that produced it.

Even work on the factory floor seemed to promise rich rewards during the industry's exuberant growing years. The big chances may have been quickly gobbled up, but with Ford's announcement of the five-dollar day in January, 1914, the millennium seemed to have dawned for workers in the industry as well. The high wage rates paid by Ford promised the factory worker what had once seemed possible only to the well-to-do. For men with an eye to independent business, such high wages offered the possibility of a quick accumulation of the necessary capital. When, under the impact of World War I, wages in other automobile plants came to equal those paid by Ford, the industry as a whole acquired a reputation for high wages. Detroit became the Mecca of the industrial worker with lesser automobile cities—Flint, Pontiac, Lansing, Toledo—as satellites. Swarms of hopeful workers came from all directions—from the South, from the farms of the Midwest and southern Ontario, from the cut-over timber areas and the depleted mining country of northern Michigan. Large groups of immigrants settled in and near Detroit to reap the fruits awaiting them in this booming new industry.

These facts of the automobile industry's early growth, embellished so as to make them seem applicable to the present, constitute in large measure the basis of the tradition of opportunity for the automobile worker. But the picture of opportunity in the industry is today very different for the capable mechanics, the would-be inventors, and the hopeful entrepreneurs who are trying to get on in the world. Indeed, the picture had started to change almost as quickly as it had become a public image.

By 1919 the boom years were over. The productive capacity of the industry, enormously multiplied by extraordinarily rapid mechanization, had run beyond the nation's capacity to consume, except perhaps for the most prosperous years. Table 2 indicates the course of production and employ-

Table 2

EMPLOYMENT AND PRODUCTION IN THE AUTOMOBILE INDUSTRY, 1919–1941

Year	Production Workers (in 000's)	Per Cent Change	Automobiles Built* (in 000's)	Per Cent Change
1919	343	. .	1,876	. .
1921	213	−38	1,616	−8
1923	427	100	4,034	174
1925	449	5	4,265	6
1927	390	−13	3,401	−20
1929	471	21	5,358	58
1931	302	−36	2,389	−55
1933	257	−15	1,902	−20
1935	408	59	3,946	106
1937	505	24	4,806	22
1939	402	−20	3,577	−26
1941	570	42	4,840	35

* Including trucks and busses.
Source: *Automobile Facts and Figures*, 28th Edition, Detroit, Automobile Manufacturers Association, 1948, pp. 4, 35.

ment between 1919 and 1941. Until 1921, when both production and employment decreased, the industry had never failed to increase its output and work force in every year of its existence, but in the following two decades both production and employment followed an erratic course with serious consequences for opportunities for individual advancement.

The end of the insatiable market intensified what had always been keen competition. As a result, most of the smaller firms were gradually forced out of business. Opportunities for men with "large visions and little capital" to embark upon independent business ventures in the automobile industry disappeared quickly as automobile manufacturing was concentrated in a few giants, each with several cars in its string, and a handful of independents. By 1923 ten companies were turning out ninety per cent of the total output of the industry. Further concentration during the twenties and the Great Depression left approximately ninety per cent of total production in the hands of the Big Three: General Motors, Ford, and Chrysler.

The war saved several independents who were on the verge of collapse, and in the years after World War II, all automobile producers, including Henry Kaiser, the only important new entry to the industry in many years,* managed to survive and in some cases to flourish. But with the renewal of intense competition in recent years, the independents have been forced to merge in order to survive as effective units in the industry. The expectation in many quarters is the eventual emergence of one large company which will include all of the present independents: Studebaker-Packard, Nash-Hudson (American Motors), and Kaiser-Willys.

Today the automobile industry cannot spell substantial opportunity to automobile workers with an eye to independence. Although General Motors claimed in 1949 that its twelve thousand parts-suppliers give evidence that opportunity is created by giant corporations (as Ford did in 1950 with its seven thousand suppliers),[10] parts production today also requires capital funds and technical skills beyond the reach of most workers, except perhaps for tool-and-die makers who may try to open a job shop to do contract work for large producers. Only in the peripheral lines—selling new or used cars, operating a gas station or an automobile-repair shop—does there seem to be room for the "little man." Yet even there the most stable and profitable field, new car sales and service, requires a capital investment far beyond the resources of the ordinary worker. In 1945, for example, the average investment of General Motors dealers was approximately twenty-five thousand

* So heavy have capital demands in the industry become that only a man with the resources of Henry Kaiser could launch a new enterprise, and even the survival of his venture, now merged with Willys-Overland, was looked upon as something of a modern wonder.

dollars, more in large cities, less in small towns.[11] It seems clear that the automobile worker clinging to the American dream of small business must look forward to some totally new field unrelated to the automobile industry or must confine himself to the modest dimensions of a filling station or repair shop. (The number of passenger-car dealers increased 8.4% between 1941 and 1953; independent repair shops increased 26.5% during the same period.)[12]

Wage rates in the automobile industry have been high ever since the inauguration of the five-dollar day in 1914,* yet automobile workers have found it difficult, on the whole, to put aside enough savings to venture into those small business fields open to them. From 1919 until the outbreak of World War II, tens of thousands of workers were laid off each year, even in times of high production, for periods that ranged up to several months in length. A 1929 report of the Bureau of Labor Statistics concluded that "the automobile industry shows the greatest instability of employment of any of the industries so far analysed by the bureau in its studies of this subject."[13] In 1939 only 35.1% of male automobile workers were employed for the full twelve months of the year, a figure lower than that for any other manufacturing industry except the hat industry.[14] Seasonal layoffs, with their hardships, were an expected part of the workers' experience, a "normal" feature of work in the automobile industry, with temporary employment difficult to secure during layoffs because of bruising competition for fill-in jobs. As is evident from Table 2, these layoffs were frequently aggravated by the marked sensitivity of automobile production to slight fluctuations of the economy. Even the introduction of installment buying after World War I and the annual model changes designed to encourage style-conscious buying could not eliminate wide fluctuations in sales and consequently in production and employment.

Only during World War II did automobile workers enjoy an extended period of uninterrupted employment. While the postwar demand for automobiles forestalled an immediate return to the extended seasonal lay-offs of the past, workers in the industry have continued to suffer from regular bouts of temporary unemployment. Changeover from one year's model to the next, carried on in the past during the annual layoff and sometimes used to justify it, has been accomplished in recent years with a minimum

---

* In 1925 average hourly earnings in the industry were $.723, compared with $.55 for all manufacturing industries. Between 1937 and 1944, average hourly earnings for automobile workers were higher than for workers in any other industry except the printing industry in 1939 and 1940. The 1925 figure is from *Monthly Labor Review* 28:178–179 (May, 1929). The 1925 figure for all manufacturing industries is from G. F. Bloom and H. R. Northrup: *Economics of Labor and Industrial Relations*, Philadelphia, The Blakiston Company, 1950, p. 68. Data for 1937 to 1944 are from *Automotive and Aviation Industries*, March 15, 1946, Statistical Issue, p. 70.

of dislocation, but strikes, material shortages, and occasional slumps in the market, have thrown men out of work for varying periods of time. For several years after the end of the war automobile workers suffered from short workweeks because of inadequate supplies of necessary materials, particularly steel. General Motors workers were on strike for four-and-a-half months during the winter of 1945–1946, while Chrysler workers were out for almost three months in 1950. Coal and railroad strikes idled virtually the entire industry on several occasions. Strikes against parts manufacturers interfered seriously with production in many large plants. Brief wildcat strikes by a few men at a time have meant that thousands were temporarily laid off until the issues affecting the small group were settled.* So dependent is automobile production upon the steady flow of raw materials and component parts that any break in delivery or production may mean anywhere from a handful to many thousands of workers will be idled for a while.

If automobile workers drop their dreams of independence because of these or other considerations and turn their attention to advancement within the plants in which they work, they face other handicaps. They are employed in large plants in which it is not easy to figure out where and how to gain promotion, in which the personal recognition that may lead to advancement is difficult to achieve. In 1939 seventy-six per cent of all automobile workers were employed in factories with over one thousand employees each, 47.6% in plants with over 2,500, and only thirteen per cent in plants with less than five hundred employees. In 1947 eighty-four per cent were in factories with over one thousand employees and sixty-four per cent in plants with over 2,500. In these large plants the gap between the managerial hierarchy and manual work in the factory is difficult to cross, while there is little room for personal advancement on the factory floor.

Both management and engineering have become highly selective, requiring men with training in universities or technical schools. Of the thirty-

* The impact of the occasional small wildcat strike is illustrated in the following news story from *The New York Times*, May 3, 1952: "DETROIT, May 2—(U.P.) At 10 A.M. today, a Chrysler worker was dismissed 'for not doing his job properly,' and this was the aftermath:

"At 12:15 P.M., seventy-five other workers in his department which makes automobile frame assemblies, walked out to protest the discharge.

"At 12:30 P.M., Chrysler was forced to send home 2,000 final assembly line workers because of the lack of frames.

"At 1 P.M., the plant across the street, which supplies auto bodies to the main plant, had to shut down, making 3,650 more workers idle.

"At 2 P.M., the whole plant went down as 1,300 shop and motor line workers were sent home.

"Total idle men: 7,000."

three top executives in General Motors in 1950, for example, twenty-four had completed either university or engineering school. Four of the other nine had had some form of post-high-school training, while only one of the remaining five started in the ranks of labor. In the early days of the industry there were, according to one chronicler of its growth, "comparatively few men in the business who held a college degree."[15] Between 1908, when the General Motors Corporation was organized, and 1919, shortly before the duPonts acquired control, only eight of nineteen top General Motors executives for whom information is available were college graduates. And the top echelons of General Motors during those years may have had more formal education than executives of other automobile companies because the Corporation was to a large extent created and directed by lawyers, bankers, and promoters who brought together going enterprises. Technical innovation, once largely the province of imaginative mechanics, is now primarily the product of organized research by well-trained scientists; in 1947 the industry employed in research activities approximately six thousand men and women whose "breeding grounds . . . are in the colleges."[16] Even plant supervision, as we shall see later, is coming more and more to demand formal education.

Despite the claim by an automobile industry economist that "a constant upgrading of individuals is normal in the industry . . . limited only by the capacity and willingness of the individual,"[17] automobile workers cannot usually look forward to any substantial personal advancement through a series of progressively more skilled and better-paid jobs. Increasing mechanization, made profitable by the enormous volume of production, has left most automobile workers as semiskilled operatives. Only a small proportion are skilled workers, while most of the heavy unskilled labor has been eliminated by machinery. As early as 1922, Henry Ford estimated that eighty-five per cent of the workers in his plants needed less than two weeks of training and that forty-three per cent could be working efficiently within one day.[18] A study by the United States Employment Service in 1935 showed that twenty-seven per cent of all automobiles workers needed no training, while only ten per cent needed more than one year.[19] On the basis of the data reported in the latest (1950) study of wages and hours in the automobile industry, it appears that about ten per cent of automobile workers are in skilled occupations.[20] It seems highly probable that most other jobs still require only a few days or weeks of training. Because most jobs do require little training, workers can move easily from one task to another in an industry whose endlessly changing technology is constantly eliminating old jobs and creating new ones. Examination of the changing job classifications used by the Bureau of Labor Statistics in its studies of wages and hours in the automobile industry provides rich evidence of the industry's changing occupational structure. But as we shall see later, it is very difficult for the ordinary nonskilled worker to gain entry to the skilled occupations except in periods of extreme labor shortage.

Since most automobile workers are engaged in semiskilled machine operation and assembly work and are paid by the hour rather than by piece rates, wages in the industry are highly compressed. In February, 1950, for example, sixty per cent of all workers in passenger-car plants earned between $1.50 and $1.70 per hour; the earnings of fifty per cent fell within a fourteen-cent range around the average.[22] (We shall be primarily concerned in this study with workers in one passenger-car plant.) In most plants, new workers start at rates slightly below the regular job rates which they reach after a ninety-day probationary period. A substantial spread between minimum and maximum hourly rates is found only in some skilled occupations.

With such limited wage differentials, most workers can hope to earn more money primarily through general wage increases. For them, opportunity in the large plants in which they work has become to a great extent a collective affair in which the union plays a major role. Advancement is less and less an individual matter and more the collective gaining and holding of standardized agreements which provide for higher wages and for other benefits such as old-age pensions, hospitalization insurance, and life insurance.

Even those opportunities for personal advancement which are available in the factory have been transformed to some extent by the union. In so far as seniority governs promotion, advancement depends upon how long a man has been on the job. The seniority rule has relegated the traditional prerequisites for advancement—effort, character, ability—to a minor role, although one may question whether these prerequisites could or did function in a large, highly mechanized automobile plant even before the advent of the union.

The disparity between tradition and reality which thus provides the context for the occupational experience and economic efforts of automobile workers can be seen clearly in the following summary comparison of ideological assertion and economic fact.

1. Each job should be looked upon as a step to something better.

But: In the factory there are few clear-cut sequences of progressively more skilled, better-paid jobs.

2. The corporation provides a "pyramid of opportunities from the bottom toward the top."

But: Executives and technicians are increasingly recruited from well-trained college and technical school graduates rather than from the ranks of factory labor. In the factory the narrow range of wage rates sets a low ceiling on possible advancement.

3. Initiative and ability inevitably lead to promotion and advancement.

But: Carefully laid-out time-studied jobs in a highly rationalized industry provide little opportunity to display either initiative or ability.

4. Success depends primarily upon each individual's efforts and capabilities.

But: Advancement within the factory is increasingly collective in character.

5. Small business provides ever-open possibilities for economic achievement.

But: Since automobile workers can at best accumulate only limited capital resources, only the riskier fields of enterprise where typically business mortality is high and profits are low are open to them.

6. Men can save enough to start a small business if they are willing to sacrifice present gratifications for future rewards.

But: Savings are frequently depleted by recurrent periods of temporary unemployment while the tendency to save is itself sharply challenged by constant stimulation to maintain a high and ever-rising standard of living.

These contrasts between reality and the promises of the tradition should not be taken as evidence of any over-all decline in vertical mobility or in workers' chances of getting ahead. We have already pointed out the difficulties which we face in arriving at definitive conclusions concerning changes in the frequency with which individuals can and do rise in American society.* Long-run changes in the automobile industry which have narrowed the avenues for advancement open to workers may have been balanced by new opportunities for workers elsewhere. Nevertheless the fact remains that automobile workers are employed in an industry which, despite its almost meteoric expansion in the past and its once-rich opportunities, now provides few chances for them to gain substantial individual advancement.

The most fruitful approach to what "opportunity" means to workers in this industry, now America's largest, lies in the analysis of the concrete alternatives they feel are open to them and the specific goals toward which they direct their attention and their energies. Do automobile workers see any opportunities for advancement in the factories in which they work or do they "look forward to remaining more or less at the same levels?" Do they see their future as confined to work in the factory or do they hope to venture into some form of independent enterprise or, perhaps, into some other alternative such as farming, selling, or civil-service employment?

* See pp. 2–3.

What do they think are the prerequisites for success in these various fields? What role do their views on how to get on in the world play in their hopes and plans.

Whether workers persist in large ambitions despite disappointment or give up their efforts to get ahead, they face the problem of maintaining self-regard and self-esteem in "a culture which continuously batters the ego of the unsuccessful."[23] Can they protect themselves in some manner from the "aspirational barrage" to which they are exposed and from the consequences of failure? Do workers who are caught between open-ended exhortation to succeed as individuals and the confining realities of working-class life reject the tradition of opportunity or do they seek to reconcile in some fashion either failure or limited aspirations with the predominant success values of American culture?

Footnotes to Chapter II

1. United States Bureau of the Census: *Statistical Abstract of the United States*, 1952, Washington, D.C., Government Printing Office, 1953, Table 943, pp. 793–795.

2. For a full analysis of the public image of Henry Ford, see K. Sward: *The Legend of Henry Ford*, New York, Rinehart & Company, Inc., 1948, particularly Chapter 21. Although much of the adulation heaped upon Ford was perhaps warranted by his particular genius, its extent, as Sward shows, was also in part the product of careful publicity.

3. D. L. Cohn: *Combustion on Wheels*, Boston, Houghton Mifflin Co., 1942, p. 83. See also R. C. Epstein: *The Automobile Industry*, New York, A. W. Shaw, 1928, p. 39.

4. L. H. Seltzer: *A Financial History of the American Automobile Industry*, Boston, Houghton Mifflin Co., 1928, p. 20.

5. E. D. Kennedy: *The Automobile Industry*, New York, Reynal & Hitchcock, 1941, pp. 82–83.

6. See Epstein, *op. cit.*, pp. 258–259.

7. Sward, *op. cit.*, pp. 55, 71.

8. For accounts of the careers of early leaders of the industry, see T. F. MacManus and N. Beasely: *Men, Money, and Motors*, New York, Harper & Brothers, 1930, and C. H. Glasscock: *The Gasoline Age*, New York, The Bobbs-Merrill Company, Inc., 1937.

9. Henry Ford: *My Life and Work*, Garden City, Doubleday, Page and Company, 1922, p. 98.

10. See *G.M. and Its People*, Detroit, General Motors Corporation, 1949, p. 8. This is a booklet prepared by General Motors both for its employees and for the general public. A series of advertisements by the Ford Motor Company early in 1950 also stressed the Company's contribution to opportunities for small business. See, for example, the Ford advertisement in *The New York Times*, January 23, 1950. The same advertisement also appeared in *Life*, January 20, 1950.

11. P. Drucker: *Concept of the Corporation*, New York, The John Day Co., 1946, p. 110.

12. *Automobile Facts and Figures*, 33rd ed., Detroit, Automobile Manufacturers Association, 1953, p. 34.

13. "Instability of Employment in the Automobile Industry," *Monthly Labor Review* 28:20–23 (February, 1929).

14. United States Bureau of the Census: *Sixteenth Census of the United States, 1940, Population, The Labor Force (Sample Statistics), Industrial Characteristics*, Washington, D.C., Government Printing Office, 1943, p. 167.

15. Glasscock, *op. cit.*, p. 245.

16. See "Auto Research Shows How," *Business Week*, October 4, 1947, pp. 72–76.

17. A. T. Court: *Men, Methods and Machines in Automobile Manufacturing*, New York, Automobile Manufacturers Association, 1939, p. 13 (Pamphlet).

18. Ford, *op. cit.*, p. 110.

19. Cited in W. H. McPherson: *Labor Relations in the Automobile Industry*, Washington, D.C., Brookings Institution, 1940, p. 9.

20. United States Department of Labor, Bureau of Labor Statistics: Bulletin No. 1015, *Wage Structure, Motor Vehicles and Parts*, 1950, Washington, D.C., Government Printing Office, 1951. The ten per cent figure is derived from an analysis of specific occupational data in the study since there is no breakdown of occupations by skill.

21. See United States Department of Labor, Bureau of Labor Statistics: Bulletin No. 348, *Wages and Hours of Labor in the Automobile Industry*, 1922; Bulletin No. 438, *Wages and Hours of Labor in the Motor-Vehicle Industry*, 1925; Bulletin No. 502, *Wages and Hours of Labor in the Motor-Vehicle Industry*, 1928; Bulletin No. 706, *Wage Structure of the Motor-Vehicle Industry*, 1940; and Bulletin No. 1015, *op. cit.* See also *Monthly Labor Review* 42:521–553 (March, 1936).

22. United States Department of Labor, Bureau of Labor Statistics: Bulletin No. 1015, *op. cit.*, pp. 1, 4.

23. R. K. Merton, M. Fiske, and A. Curtis: *Mass Persuasion*, New York, Harper & Brothers, 1946, p. 160.

III

Studying Autotown's Workers

The research for this study was conducted in a middle-sized midwestern city we shall call Autotown. It covered a period of fourteen months, from August, 1946, to July, 1947, plus the summer months of 1948, and a short period in 1951. Detailed data were secured in seventy-eight prolonged interviews with sixty-two automobile workers employed in a plant which is part of one of the industry's Big Three. A small sample was chosen so that the investigation could probe deeply into men's aspirations; qualitative richness was desired rather than statistical coverage. The research was limited to men living in or near one community and working in one factory so that it would be possible to appraise in some detail how specific institutions influenced men's hopes and ambitions. The data drawn from these interviews were supplemented by a few weeks of work in the factory, by reports from informants, and by innumerable hours of casual conversation and informal social participation with workers from the plant.

Autotown, in 1946 a city of almost ninety thousand, was chosen for two reasons. First, it is an automobile city whose history has been closely linked with the development of the automobile industry. Second, its size, location, and population composition make it a less complex setting for research into the problems of opportunity and aspirations than any of the other automobile cities.

Although it contains a large number of governmental offices and is a marketing center for the surrounding rural territory, Autotown is primarily an automobile manufacturing city; its life centers around its automobile plants. In May, 1946, shortly before the research was begun, fifty-three per cent of all workers employed by firms reporting to the United States Employment Service were in the automobile industry. Almost ten thousand workers were employed in the plant from which those to be interviewed were drawn and another plant in the city which was part of the same corporation. Two smaller factories, one chiefly a truck manufacturer, the other an automobile parts producer, each employed over two thousand men. In addition, there were several small truck manufacturers, a few producers of small parts, and six drop forges and several small tool-and-die shops, most of whose output was used by the automobile industry. Eighty per cent of all workers employed in manufacturing were in the four large plants, while eleven per cent were in the small plants which were part of or linked to the automobile industry.

Autotown's growth to its present size was largely the result of the expansion of the automobile industry. In 1900 the city's population was only 16,500. In 1902 one automobile plant was built, two years later another. As these plants expanded and parts plants to supply them and automobile producers elsewhere were established, they drew workers many of whom had hopes of cashing in on the high wages and rich opportunities held out by the new industry. By 1910 the population had risen to 31,200, by 1920 to 57,300. During the twenties, another large plant was built in the city as part of a now-defunct firm; this large handsome modern factory is now one of the two plants which are part of one of the industry's giants. By 1930 the city's population had reached 78,400, a figure that remained virtually unchanged until war-generated industrial expansion stimulated further growth.

Compared with other automobile centers, Autotown has probably always possessed greater stability and promise for its workers. One of the automobile plants which played a leading role in the community's economic life until almost 1930, now chiefly a truck manufacturer, was, according to a history of the city, primarily an Autotown institution since nearly all the stockholders were residents of the city. For many years, this plant, through its apprentice program, provided the city with most of its skilled labor and was looked upon as a very desirable place to work, although its status has sunk in the last twenty years. Most of the city's leading fortunes came from local automobile plants; the city's largest public hall, its biggest hotel and office building, and one of its leading hospitals bear the names of men who gained their prominence and wealth in Autotown's automobile industry. One of the city's sons gained national prominence as a glowing example of the American success story while still retaining his ties to his home town. In the present generation of company executives there are a few men who are known as "local boys" who began in the factory and worked their way up the ladder. It is probably in part because of these facts that industrial conflict has never been waged as bitterly in Autotown as in many other automobile centers.

Part of the city's greater stability and promise undoubtedly stems from the presence of a large state-supported college in one of its suburbs and a large number of government offices in the city itself. Government is

Autotown's second "industry," employing more than six thousand men and women in 1946. Nothing precise is known about the influence of such factors as the presence of an easily accessible state university and of a middle-class public bureaucracy upon the working-class population of an industrial city. It seems likely, however, that their presence may make the city seem a better place in which to live and work and may encourage hope among workers, if not for themselves, then at least for their children.

The other characteristics which dictated the selection of Autotown promised to simplify the research problem. Autotown is not so large that a single investigator could not gain some understanding of its significant features as a setting for work and living. Located about eighty miles from the nearest major city, Autotown is relatively free from metropolitan domination. Metropolitan newspapers are sold in Autotown and metropolitan radio and television programs are popular there, but the city does have its own daily paper and its own radio stations, and it is not dependent upon its larger neighbor for shopping or other institutional facilities.

Analysis of differences in the aspirations of various racial and ethnic groups was deliberately excluded by the choice of Autotown, since ninety-three per cent of its population in 1940 consisted of native-born whites. In 1930, 69.5% of its population had been children of native-born white parents; although the 1940 census did not provide a comparable figure, this percentage had probably increased by that time. In 1946, even after a major influx of Negroes, there were only about five thousand of them in the city, or about 5.5% of the city's total. (In 1940 there had been only 1,600 Negroes in the city.)

The final decision to carry on the research in Autotown was made, however, only after the cooperation of a large local of the United Automobile Workers union was secured. The cooperation of the union alone, rather than of management alone, or of both, was solicited because there seemed reason for doubting that the cooperation of both management and union could be secured for this particular project. (At a later stage in the study, however, some company executives were interviewed.) Joint cooperation was not essential since the study was not focussed on collective bargaining; assistance of the union appeared to be more important in this case than that of management. Another possibility would have been to ignore both management and union and to approach workers directly. This alternative, however, offered no positive advantages while it would have lost whatever could be gained by developing close relationships with either or both union and management.

Acceptance of the investigator by factory workers was the major research requirement; any identification that might have created suspicion had to be avoided. Even if management were willing to cooperate fully with an investigator who was also working closely with the union, as they probably would have been, there was some doubt that rank-and-file workers and local union officers would feel at ease with someone who was close to management and who, in addition, might induce suspicion because of his own status and personal background. Labor relations in the automobile industry have not been such as to create a sympathetic attitude toward management on the part of workers except, perhaps, in recent years. In a preliminary discussion of research procedures a high official of the U.A.W. warned: "Don't be found dead near a personnel man." Although perhaps an overstatement which is more indicative of the sentiments of some union officials than of rank-and-file workers, this warning did find some support in the tentative suspicion and distrust elicited by my presence, my interest, and my questions, and in the attitudes toward management which were occasionally expressed. It seems likely that the cooperation of union officials and of many workers would not have been as extensive as it was had an attempt been made to gain joint union and management sponsorship. This fact, in the writer's judgment, compensated for the absence of explicit and continuing aid and support from management.

The assistance and backing of high-ranking U.A.W. officials were enlisted early in the planning stage of the study. They suggested that the work be done in Autotown, where the officers of one particular local union, they felt, would probably be responsive to the proposed research. Leaders of the local were then approached; the purpose of the study was explained to them and their assistance requested. Although they agreed to participate from the first, their active cooperation came only after an informal probationary period during which my words and actions were closely watched and evaluated.

A detailed description of the process by which the cooperation of the local union leaders and of active rank-and-file members was gained is not necessary here. But two steps which facilitated relations with the men with whom I came into frequent contact should be noted. I went to work in the plant as a manual worker and joined the union.

A job in the plant was part of the original research plan; since 1946 was a time of labor shortage and high turnover, there was no difficulty in securing employment in the factory. Only a few weeks were spent in the plant, however, because it soon became evident that the circumstances of work on the assembly line to which I was assigned made it difficult to talk to other men or to pay attention to much more than the work itself. It therefore seemed more profitable to center time and effort upon interviews after men had finished their day's work. The few weeks in the shop were useful as an introduction to factory problems and to workers' jargon, as a source of fruitful hypotheses, and as a basis for establishing rapport with workers who were subsequently interviewed. The fact that I had punched a time clock and worked on the assembly line also allayed whatever doubts may have existed about me among union officials and active members. And union membership was the conclusive warrant to these men of my sincerity; without it I should still have remained suspect.

My role in relation to the union officials and members was that of a sympathetic observer who was trying to understand the life and problems of automobile workers. There was no denial of middle-class status, although working in the shop did break down some of the distinctions men might make. As a once-antagonistic union official phrased his version of my role in a letter of introduction to a union officer in another city: "He worked in our shop to gather a lot of his necessary knowledge, so he is not just a 'Professor,' he is actually a 'Worker.'" By further stressing the fact that I was a learner in this situation, the possibility of resentment at imagined condescension was lessened and the flow of relevant information was encouraged, even to the point where an occasional worker sought me out with the comment: "Here's something you ought to know. . . ."

Union officials provided information about workers in the plant, about the background of work in the factory, and about the community. They helped to secure interviews by suggesting possible respondents and by vouching for my reliability and trustworthiness. "I called the union hall," said one worker when I arrived for a scheduled interview, "because I didn't know what I ought to say to you and they told me to answer any questions you might ask." The union also offered an institutional avenue for coming to know many men quite well; the better-informed and more perceptive workers served as informants with whom observations could be checked and from whom new observations could be elicited. And, of course, the union itself was an institution whose influence upon workers' aspirations was to be examined.

Names of workers to be interviewed were secured in various ways. Initially a random sample was drawn from the union register; in order to include workers not in the union an additional list was made from those who had formally withdrawn from the union in the preceding six months according to a procedure specified in the contract. It soon appeared, however, that this sample would be confined largely to men with long seniority and to workers over thirty years of age, probably because of a high rate of turnover among younger, recently hired workers, many of whom were recently discharged veterans. In their short tenure in the factory, many of these men did not join the union and were therefore missed in a sample drawn from union files. Other ways of choosing workers to be interviewed therefore were needed. Since no effort was made to enlist the cooperation of the company, its personnel records were not available; the union possessed no complete, classified list of workers from which a representative sample could have been chosen. The initial list taken from the union records was therefore supplemented by names suggested by union officials and, in later stages of the study, by men who were themselves interviewed. In securing the names of additional respondents an effort was made to include a substantial number in each of the various age, job, and seniority groups, since it seemed likely that these factors would have considerable influence upon workers' aspirations.

The age, seniority, and type of work of the sixty-two men who were formally interviewed are shown in Tables 3 and 4. Since age and seniority are obviously related, they are combined in Table 3. Thirteen men were under thirty, twenty-three between thirty and thirty-nine, thirteen in their

Table 3

AGE AND SENIORITY OF WORKERS INTERVIEWED

| Age | Seniority | | | Totals |
	Before 1941	1941–Aug., 1945	After Aug., 1945	
20–29	..	5	8	13
30–39	15	6	2	23
40–49	9	3	1	13
50–over	11	1	1	13
Totals	35	15	12	62

forties, and thirteen were fifty or over. Thirty-five workers had been employed in the plant since 1940 or earlier, fifteen had been hired between 1941 and the end of the war in August, 1945, and twelve had come into the plant after that date. Thirteen men had worked in the plant on various occasions before their most recent hiring, from which their seniority was calculated. The large number of prewar employees was not disproportionate since in September, 1946, 53.6% of the workers in the plant had prewar seniority.

The job classifications used in Table 4 are based on the distinctions made by the workers themselves in their discussion of jobs in the shop. The line between unskilled and semiskilled is not easy to draw in the modern automobile plant and hardly enters into workers' classification of jobs. They differentiate between *skilled* and *nonskilled*, but in the latter category they separate *production* jobs, which include assembly-line tasks, machine operation, and various miscellaneous classifications, from *off-production* jobs which include inspection, maintenance, and shipping. These latter jobs

Table 4

JOBS HELD BY WORKERS INTERVIEWED

Skilled		15 (including one apprentice)
Nonskilled		
Production		29
Assembly line	9	
Machine operation	10	
Others	10	
Off-production		18
Total		62

do not involve actual fabrication of parts or assembly of the finished product. Fifteen of the workers interviewed were skilled, twenty-nine held various production jobs, and eighteen were doing off-production work.

Since there might be differences in the aspirations of union and non-union members, eleven men who did not belong to the union were included among the sixty-two who were interviewed. The number of active union members who were interviewed was kept low, since only a small proportion of members participate actively in union affairs. Four of those interviewed were shop stewards, two were alternate stewards who were not active in union affairs. Four others who fell into the research net had been stewards in the past but no longer participated in union activities except for occasional attendance at a union meeting.

Other characteristics which may have some bearing on workers' aspirations should also be noted here. Virtually all the workers who were interviewed came from working-class or lower-middle-class families. Fourteen were sons of skilled workers, twenty-four of unskilled or semiskilled laborers, and ten came from farm families. In ten cases, the father had been a small business man, a white-collar employee, or, in the case of one toolmaker, a doctor. No data were available in four cases.

In order to simplify the research problem, interviews were confined almost completely to native-born whites.* All but six were married. Seventeen men had been born in Autotown, thirty-three came from small towns or from rural areas in the state, and two from small towns elsewhere in the Midwest. Three had moved to Autotown from large cities, one as a child, two as adults. Three were foreign-born. The origins of four were not ascertained.

---

* Three workers were sons of foreign-born parents, one from Poland, one from the Ukraine, one from French Canada. One worker had been brought from Italy at the age of two. One was a Scottish coal-miner who had come to the United States when he was twenty. And one was a fifty-three-year-old Canadian who had come to Autotown as a young man in order to work in the automobile industry.

Twenty-two of the sixty-two workers had completed high school; two of these had had some college training and two others had graduated from small colleges in the state. Twenty-three had had some high-school education but had never graduated. Fifteen had not gone beyond the eighth grade. In two cases no data on education were secured.

Despite the unsystematic procedures for securing interviews, there does not appear to be any obvious statistical bias in the group interviewed. There is, however, one important gap in the coverage. All but one of the sixty-two workers lived in the city or in adjacent suburbs. With one exception, the approximate one-third of all workers who lived in the surrounding small towns or on nearby farms were unrepresented. The influence of rural residence upon aspirations cannot, therefore, be adequately assessed. Informal discussions with some out-of-town workers were carried on in the union hall occasionally, but complete data could not be secured from these men under such circumstances.

In each interview an attempt was made to secure personal information: age, education, family background, and job experience, and to discuss the worker's attitudes toward the job he held, his hope or expectation of advancement in the shop, alternatives outside the factory which he might be considering, feelings about management and the union, ambitions for children, beliefs about opportunity and advancement, and general orientation toward present and future. Interviews ranged in length from half an hour to a maximum of four hours, although most of them lasted from an hour to an hour and a half.*

The difficulties inherent in the attempt to interview manual workers intensively in their homes about problems which may carry heavy emotional loadings give such work an almost inevitably uneven character. Contours of interviews varied from one individual to another because of problems in the interview situation or because of inevitable variations in workers' ability and willingness to talk about their experience and their feelings. Most interviews were held in workers' homes; since these were usually small four- or five-room bungalows, someone else was occasionally present. In most cases it was the worker's wife; in several cases friends were there when the interview started or came in during the course of the conversation. The presence of others obviously made it difficult to raise some questions and

---

* Notes were taken during most interviews and were used to record each interview in as complete detail as possible. In order to insure maximum recall and accuracy, each interview was recorded as soon as possible. No interview was conducted until the preceding one was already transcribed. Although complete verbatim records were therefore not available, the transcription of each interview did tend to follow the phrasing and vocabulary of the men interviewed. In a few cases in which it appeared that note-taking inhibited conversation, pencil and notebook were laid aside and the interview later recorded from memory.

to discuss others fully. In these circumstances, discussion was centered on the more or less objective problems of the character of opportunity, the requisites for advancement in the shop, and union and management policies, rather than on the attitudes of the worker toward himself and his future.

Not enough time was available in some cases to discuss all the topics on which information was needed, despite the fact that all interviews were arranged in advance. The study was described to prospective respondents as a survey of the problems of automobile workers and of their attitudes toward these problems. Only a small number refused to cooperate, although some others had set aside a very short time despite the advance warning that the interview would require about an hour. When it appeared that time would run out before all the desired data were secured, the most promising leads were followed up in detail, while others were neglected. This procedure seemed warranted by the intensive, qualitative character of the investigation. In twelve cases it was possible to arrange follow-up interviews, but in a number of others there were gaps in the available information.

Most of the men who were interviewed responded freely and willingly to questions in spite of the difficulties that sometimes intruded into the interview situation. But two markedly different responses which created problems of interview procedure and of interpretation and analysis could sometimes be distinguished when discussion touched on matters of direct personal concern. Some men closed up completely, obviously unwilling to talk about possibly painful topics. Occasionally this withdrawal was easily perceptible, but in other cases one could not know whether disavowal of interest was authentic or was merely avoidance of emotionally loaded problems. When such an interpretive question arose, for example, when workers said that they had never thought of the possibility of becoming foremen, the topic was approached again later in the interview in some other way in order to confirm the expressed lack of interest or to break down any emotional blocks to free expression of attitude and feeling which might exist.

Emotionally loaded subjects sometimes produced the opposite response; some men seized greedily the opportunity to talk about matters of intense personal interest. In such cases these topics tended to dominate the conversation and to preclude discussion of other subjects. When relevant to the research problem, this was useful, as in the case of the toolmaker who discussed his plans for starting a tool-and-die shop for the better part of a two-hour interview. When the subject of pressing concern to the worker was unrelated or tangential to the research problem, when, for example, one worker tried to convert the investigator to his particular form of evangelical Christianity, the research value of the interview was obviously diminished.

As new insights emerged from the accumulating mass of data, leading to new hypotheses or suggesting alternative lines of inquiry, the content of subsequent interviews tended to change. New questions were added in order to provide data to test new hypotheses; to make room for these new questions, old ones which were of lesser value or which had provided enough data for tentative conclusions were dropped. Changes in the content of interviews are most clear-cut between July, 1947, when the first period of research ended, and the summer of 1948, when some additional interviews were conducted in order to fill gaps which had become apparent in the earlier material.

Finally, in order to analyse adequately the nature and functions of workers' views of opportunity in the factory, it was necessary to secure an objective description of the structure and operations of the plant. Interviews with management officials, discussions with union officers, and an examination of the union contract and other documents provided that description of the structure of opportunity in the factory.

Changes which have occurred since the bulk of the data were secured in 1946, 1947, and 1948 may have affected the patterns of workers' aspirations. New union contracts have increased workers' protection against the hazards of sickness and accident and have provided some degree of assurance against threatening old age. The fluctuations of the economy during the past five years have alternately offered new opportunities and created temporary unemployment and job insecurity. (The automobile industry, as we noted earlier, is particularly susceptible to the ups and downs of the business cycle.) * And the pervasive anxieties of the Atomic Age may be having cumulative and lasting effects upon workers' aims and ambitions.

The reader of the following chapters, therefore, should remember that they apply to post–World War II America, when veterans were still finding their way back into the economy in large numbers, when the Taft-Hartley Act was under debate, when a runaway inflation threatened as the nation wavered between postwar depression and postwar boom. Despite the changes which have occurred, however, and the immediate historical context which inevitably influences how men view the opportunities open to them, this study suggests the varied elements which in one form or another enter into workers' aims and aspirations in a big-business-dominated industrial society.

---

* See pp. 17–18.

IV

The Factory: The Structure of Opportunity

We have suggested that American society, with careless disregard for class differences in access to opportunity and for individual differences in ability, energy, or drive, encourages all men to pattern their aspirations in terms of steady economic advancement. It offers no definition of what is "enough" since all ranges of wealth are putatively within the reach of everyone.

We have seen that in the modern automobile plant workers' ambitions and desires are caught in two coercive processes: the steadily increasing mechanization of production and the marked separation of management and labor. Not only have these processes narrowed the range of opportunity open to most manual workers, but they have also concentrated intelligence and control in the hands of technicians and executives and have therefore left workers with little chance to exercise judgment, assume responsibility, or develop significant skills. The routine tasks performed by most workers lend themselves to constant rationalization by engineers and time-study men. Routinized jobs and a standardized wage structure take away men's uniqueness and reduce them to anonymous entities who can be easily managed and manipulated in accordance with the needs of a constantly changing mechanical technology.

The aspirations of workers must be seen in relation to the concrete alternatives open to them in this industrial context. These alternatives are defined by the objective characteristics of the plant in which they work: its formal organization, job classifications, wage structure, and operating rules.

The A.B.C. plant, as we shall label it, is both a parts-producer and an assembly plant. A considerable proportion of the motors, fenders, hoods, axles, and other parts it manufactures are shipped to other plants of the Corporation for assembly, while simultaneously a steady flow of finished automobiles comes from its own assembly lines. Locked into the inter-dependent technology of a mass-production industry, A.B.C. feeds other plants at the same time that it is dependent upon others for important

34

items such as bodies and frames and for a host of smaller parts needed in the assembly of the finished product.

The A.B.C. plant consists of nine divisions: axle and final assembly, motor and crankshaft, sheet metal and paint, maintenance, inspection, material-handling, tool and die, parts and service, and experimental and engineering. The first three divisions, taken together, constitute what is called "automotive production." Workers in the other divisions distribute materials and supplies, prepare tools and dies needed in production and repair them when necessary, inspect the work as it comes out of a machine or off the assembly line, keep the machinery in working order and the plant clean, ship out parts and completed cars, and assist in the experimental and engineering work devoted to the development of new machines and new automobile models.*

Slightly over sixty per cent of the approximately six thousand workers in the plant were engaged in automotive production. Five per cent were in the inspection division, ten per cent in parts and service, and nine per cent in material-handling. Tool and die and the maintenance division each accounted for six per cent of the total, while only two per cent were in experimental and engineering. A very small proportion of workers such as timekeepers, janitors, and some laborers were not assigned to any one division.

The formal organization of the plant into divisions, however, is perhaps less important in relation to workers' job goals than the kinds of jobs which men hold. Exact figures on the number of men doing the various types of work in the factory were not available, but some rough estimates can be made. About a quarter of all workers were tied to some kind of conveyor line.† Most line workers were engaged in the assembly of a major component such as the motor or axle, or of the finished product on the final assembly line, although other operations such as painting and finishing fenders and hoods were also performed by men who remained stationed in one place, doing their repetitive tasks while the materials moved past on an endless conveyor belt.

Approximately thirty per cent of the workers were operating automatic or semiautomatic machines such as drill presses, milling machines, lathes, boring machines, grinders, or chucking machines. These are all repetitive

---

* The major research activities of the Corporation as a whole are concentrated in its Research Laboratories Division, but each plant or division does some research as well as its own engineering development.

† This estimate was made by the plant's Personnel Director. Except for a record of the number of skilled workers and the organization of most inspectors into one division, management has no figures on the number of workers engaged in various kinds of tasks such as line assembly, machine operation, bench assembly, etc.

tasks, although they vary in the demands they make of workers. The simplest of them require only that the worker insert a piece or pieces of metal or semifinished parts, start the machine, and remove the parts when the operation is completed. Other machine-operators, who may need several days or weeks of training, must change tools, set their machines, and use gauges or micrometers to check the size of the finished pieces. Most of these semiskilled machine jobs were in the three divisions which constitute automotive production, although a few were to be found in other divisions of the plant as well.

Probably fifteen per cent of the workers were engaged in various other nonskilled production jobs such as welding, riveting, bench assembly, and repair work on imperfectly assembled units.

Only about three hundred men, five per cent of the total, were skilled workers. This group can be roughly divided into skilled maintenance workers such as millwrights, electricians, carpenters, machine-repair men, pipefitters, plumbers and painters, and others such as toolmakers, die-makers, pattern-makers, jig-builders, and blacksmiths.

The other twenty-five per cent of the workers in the factory were engaged in various "off-production" jobs, as they were commonly labeled. The largest single group of off-production workers consisted of inspectors, about five per cent of the total. With the exception of the very small number who inspect skilled work, inspectors are only semiskilled workers whose wages are about the same as those of most other nonskilled men. Their duties are repetitive, sometimes involving the use of automatic or semi-automatic machines, sometimes requiring merely visual or tactile examination of the parts being inspected.

The remaining off-production workers performed a wide variety of tasks which defy any simple classification. In parts and service there are clerks, stock-pickers, stock-loaders, trim-shop attendants, unitizors (who pack single parts for shipment), and scale men. In material-handling there are oil-and-paint-room attendants, conveyor attendants, crane-operators and crane-hookers, crib attendants, power-truck drivers, stock-chasers, and hand-truckers. In the maintenance division there are helpers to the various skilled workers as well as incinerator attendants, oilers, saw-filers, battery-service men, and scale-maintenance men. A relatively small number of men do the menial tasks of sweepers, janitors, chip-haulers, window cleaners, and elevator-operators, and there are a few clerks and time-keepers who are paid hourly wages and therefore are included with the factory work force rather than with the office staff. Most of those performing menial laboring tasks and clerical work in the factory were not assigned to a particular division.

As we shall see in Chapter VI, these rough distinctions among various types of work play an important part in shaping workers' job goals in the factory. The significance of these distinctions is markedly enhanced by the fact that wage rates in the plant were compressed within a narrow range despite the extensive division of labor. (There were more than five hundred separate job classifications for which hourly wage rates were set.) The extent of the relative uniformity of wage rates is indicated in Table 5 which shows, by divisions, the number of classifications with given hourly wage rates (as of May, 1947). No jobs in the plant carried piecework rates. In automotive production, which included sixty-two per cent of all workers in the plant, 181 of 206 job classifications paid maximum hourly wages of from $1.41 to $1.50. Twenty-nine of the thirty-two classifications in inspection fell within the same narrow range, as did thirty of the forty-two jobs in material-handling. In the tool-and-die, maintenance, and experimental and engineering divisions, with fourteen per cent of all workers and virtually all those with skilled trades, the range in wage rates was much greater. Only fifty-one of the total of 195 job classifications paid $1.50 per hour or less, ten jobs paid maximum rates of $1.52 to $1.60 per hour, forty-five paid $1.64 to $1.75, and seventy-seven paid maximum rates of $1.79 per hour or more, ranging up to $2.30 per hour for draftsmen in the tool-and-die division. (The large number of highly paid classifications in the tool-and-die division is the result of a high degree of specialization in the assignments of tool-and-die-makers and other skilled workers.) In parts and service and

Table 5

NUMBER OF JOB CLASSIFICATIONS BY HOURLY WAGE RATES
AND BY DIVISIONS (1947)

Division	Maximum Hourly Wage Rates						Total	% of all workers
	1.19–1.29	1.32–1.39	1.41–1.50	1.52–1.60	1.64–1.75	1.79–over		
Automotive production*	2	1	181	18	3	1	206	62
Inspection	0	0	29	1	2	0	32	5
Material-handling	4	6	30	1	1	0	42	9
Maintenance	1	12	16	7	21	11	68	6
Tool and die	0	2	6	2	13	53	76	6
Experimental and engineering	1	1	12	13	11	13	51	2
Parts and service	0	11	4	4	1	0	20	} 10
Miscellaneous	8	1	7	1	0	0	17	}
Totals	16	34	285	47	52	78	512	100

* Separate data for the three divisions which comprise automotive production were not available.

among the miscellaneous jobs in the plant there was also a wider range of maximum hourly rates than in automotive production, although the distribution is skewed somewhat toward the lower end of the wage scale.

For roughly three-fifths of the job classifications in the factory, covering about eighty per cent of all workers, maximum hourly rates were ten cents above the minimum and were automatically reached ninety days after a worker was hired. According to the contract between the Corporation and the union:

> New employees shall be hired at a rate no lower than ten cents below the rate of the job classification and shall receive an automatic increase of five cents at the expiration of thirty days. Every employee who is retained by the Corporation in the job classification shall receive an increase to the rate for the job classification within ninety days or as soon as he or she can meet the standard requirements for an average employee on the job, whichever occurs first, provided however, that deviation from the above rule may be made pursuant to negotiations between the local Shop Committee and local Managements, for jobs requiring more than ninety days to attain average proficiency.
>
> The foregoing paragraph shall not apply to tool and die rooms or to any job classification previously covered by upgrading agreements.*

In jobs covered by this contract provision, wage increases were, as a matter of practice, usually given at the end of the thirty- and ninety-day periods rather than as soon as "average proficiency" was reached. Most of the exceptions to this rule were skilled jobs which had a wage spread between minimum and maximum rates of fifteen, twenty, or twenty-one cents. The top rate for these classifications was not reached automatically after a specified time interval, however, but depended upon the discretion of the foreman. There were a few exceptions to the ten-cent spread among nonskilled jobs, as is evident from Table 6, which indicates the wage spread for all job classifications in each division. Nonskilled as well as skilled workers in the experimental and engineering, tool-and-die, and maintenance divisions enjoyed a wider-than-average wage spread. In the maintenance division, thirteen helpers to skilled workers were paid fixed hourly wages from the start without any thirty- or ninety-day increases.

Of the twenty-eight exceptions to the ten-cent spread in automotive production, inspection, material-handling, parts and service, and miscellaneous classifications, nine were group leaders, workers who were given minor supervisory responsibilities over a small group. (Only one of these nine was in automotive production, three were in material-handling, and five were in parts and service.) The union contract permitted exceptions to the automatic ten-cent-increase rule when more than ninety days were required to attain reasonable proficiency, but the remaining nineteen ex-

---

* For a discussion of upgrading, see pp. 42–43.

Table 6

NUMBER OF JOB CLASSIFICATIONS BY DIFFERENCE BETWEEN
MINIMUM AND MAXIMUM WAGE RATES, BY DIVISIONS (1947)

Division	Difference in Cents per Hour between Minimum and Maximum Wage Rates						
	.00	.10	.15	.20	.21	Total	% of all workers
Automotive production	0	194	12	0	0	206	62
Inspection	0	29	3	0	0	32	5
Material-handling	0	38*	4	0	0	42	9
Maintenance	13	7	4	0	44	68	6
Tool and die	0	0	14	62	0	76	6
Experimental and engineering	0	2	31	18	0	51	2
Parts and service	0	17	3	0	0	20	10
Miscellaneous	0	11*	6	0	0	17	
	13	298	77	80	44	512	100

* One classification does not receive the ten-cent increase automatically, but at the discretion of the foreman.

ceptions did not uniformly pay the higher wage rates that would seem to
indicate greater skill. Nine jobs paid maximum rates of $1.49 or less, one
paid $1.55, four paid $1.59, one $1.60, three $1.64, and one $1.79.

Promotion to a job that carried a higher wage rate was governed by the
seniority rule, except for entry to the skilled trades. According to the union
contract:

> In the advancement of employees to higher paid jobs when ability, merit
> and capacity are equal, employees with the longest seniority will be given
> preference.

Seniority was calculated by divisions and by groups of related jobs within
divisions labeled as "non-interchangeable occupational groups." These
groups contained an average of four or five job classifications, although
many consisted of only one classification and a few contained twenty to
thirty classifications. Similar jobs in different parts of the plant were not
lumped together; instead each group was confined to jobs within a single
department or division. Some men working in the same classification in the
same or different divisions therefore find themselves in different occupational groups. As a result, there were over 150 different non-interchangeable occupational groups in the plant. If a job opening occurred, the worker
with the longest seniority in the group was entitled to promotion. If the
opening occurred in a one-job group, or was the lowest-paid job in the
group, then the worker with the longest seniority in the division was en-

titled to it if, in comparison with others, "merit, ability and capacity were equal."

Management in the A.B.C. plant, as in most automobile plants,[1] has tried to limit the operation of the seniority rule only to those cases in which merit and competence are clearly equal. By reserving to itself the right to appraise the abilities of its employees, it could maintain a wide range of discretion in promoting workers. The union, on the other hand, has sought to enforce the seniority rule as long as the worker with the greatest service is competent to do the job. Since the union contract permitted workers to file grievances if they felt that they had been unjustifiably by-passed, any attempt to promote a worker out of the line of seniority was likely to be challenged, and such a grievance was usually pressed vigorously by the union. Detailed data on the operation of the seniority rule in A.B.C. are not available, but it did appear that in most cases promotion was based upon seniority. The possibility of a large number of grievances may itself deter management in its efforts to limit the application of the seniority rule. Since grievances can be carried to an impartial umpire who usually insists that management show substantial evidence as to the greater merit of its candidates for promotion,[2] management has tended to adhere to seniority unless it has felt that a particular decision to ignore it would be upheld if it came before the umpire.

Whatever success the union has had in limiting management's freedom to promote workers as it sees fit has been possible only because of the low level of skill and the relatively short training time required for most jobs. There are differences in proficiency in the performance even of routine tasks, but most workers can meet the minimum standards set by management for most nonskilled jobs in a fairly short time. Management's claim that one worker is better than another has been countered, more or less successfully, by the assertion that the man with the longest seniority should be given the opportunity to show if he can meet the requirements of the job. As Harbison has pointed out, the insistence of most unions upon seniority as the basis for promotion has stemmed in large part from management's inability or failure to develop explicit criteria of merit and fair and objective measures of competence.[3]

Seniority obviously can not and does not apply to entry to the skilled trades whose clearly defined job techniques cannot be easily or quickly acquired. Workers either have or do not have the necessary skills. The chances of gaining entry to any of the skilled trades depend, therefore, primarily upon the opportunities for acquiring the requisite knowledge and skills. The plant does not provide for the incoming worker a succession of progressively more demanding tasks which lead to journeyman status. There is a substantial gap between skilled and nonskilled jobs, so that workers who want to become craftsmen must either serve a formal apprenticeship or must rely upon chance opportunities to pick up all or part of the skills of some trade.

Formal apprentice training in the A.B.C. plant was virtually nonexistent until late in the thirties. Before that time the plant drew its skilled workers primarily from men who had served an apprenticeship in some other plant* or from men who had managed to acquire trade skills in some informal manner. The inauguration of formal training in the A.B.C. plant was part of a national revival of apprenticeship which began late in the depression decade and gained substantial momentum after the war.[4] With the steady mechanization of production lessening the demand for skilled labor during the 1920 decade and the depression providing an excess of labor of all kinds during the thirties, the ratio of apprentices to skilled workers in American industry reached an all-time low just before the war. In 1940 the ratio of apprentices to journeymen machinists, millwrights, toolmakers and diemakers was only 3.4 per hundred compared to a ratio of 18.6 per hundred in 1900.[5] But as production revived and the average age of skilled workers increased to the point where the problem of replacements became acute, industry as a whole and A.B.C. among others turned back to apprenticeship to provide a steady flow of well-trained skilled workers.

For most men already at work in the factory, apprentice training was out of the question. The number of apprentices was small, limited by the union contract to a maximum of one for every ten journeymen.† At the end of 1947 there were only seventeen apprentices in training. Even if men were willing to accept the immediate financial sacrifices which apprenticeship would entail (at 1947 wage rates it would have taken an apprentice toolmaker approximately eighteen months to reach the wage level of assembly-line workers), most of them would not have been able to meet the age and educational requirements. Applicants for apprentice training must be high school graduates between the ages of eighteen and twenty-one, although the age limit was relaxed after the war to permit veterans who were not yet twenty-five years old when they entered the armed forces to

---

* Seven of the skilled workers who were interviewed had learned their trades as apprentices, although none had served an apprenticeship in the A.B.C. plant. One man included in the group of skilled workers interviewed was serving his apprenticeship.

† The union has endorsed apprentice training in order to prevent abuses in the hiring and utilization of "learners" and "helpers" who could be paid minimum wages while nominally learning a skilled trade, but who could be assigned tasks normally performed by fully qualified workers. For a full-scale exposition of the union's attitude toward apprenticeship, see U.A.W.-C.I.O. International Education Department: *Apprenticeship and the U.A.W.*, Detroit, U.A.W.-C.I.O., 1941 (Pamphlet).

apply. Apprenticeship was thus automatically ruled out when workers passed their twenty-second birthday, even if they had completed high school. Only seventeen of the forty-seven nonskilled workers who were interviewed had completed high school.*

Even in the past, however, apprentice training had not provided all the skilled workers who were needed, and the present apprentice program in A.B.C. can fill only part of its needs,† particularly since only a limited number of trades are covered: toolmaking, diemaking, machine repair, electrical work, sheet-metal work and wood-model-making. Recruitment of workers in other skilled trades must continue to draw upon men trained elsewhere or upon men without formal training.

There have always been workers who managed to pick up trade skills without undergoing apprentice training and there were many such in the plant. But rules established by collective bargaining have made it difficult for employees to acquire journeyman skills without formal training. Helpers, for example, who could once hope to learn the trades of the men under whom they worked, must now perform only those duties assigned to workers in their classifications; otherwise they would be engaged in tasks which call for higher wages and would be taking work away from skilled employees. Only in small plants, where rigid job classifications do not exist or are not adhered to closely, is it possible today for workers to become skilled via an informal and casual training process.

This hitherto informal alternative to apprentice training was systematically utilized during the war in order to enable industry to meet the demands for skilled labor. In the A.B.C. plant about a thousand line assemblers, machine-operators, truck-drivers, and other nonskilled workers were transformed through on-the-job training into skilled labor. No effort was made to train "all-around mechanics"; instead these "upgraders," as they were called, were taught one part of a journeyman's job, since the volume of production made possible the splitting of skilled jobs into several narrowly defined specialties. Some upgraders did manage to extend their skills by acquiring several specialties within a single trade. A small number

* As the proportion of American youth who graduate from high school increases, there will probably be a steady increase in the proportion of automobile workers who have graduated from high school. Thirteen of the seventeen nonskilled workers who had completed high school were thirty-three years old or less, compared with only eight of the twenty-nine who had not completed high school. No information was available in one case.

† In industry as a whole it has been estimated that "replacements needed to maintain the skilled labor force at a constant level are . . . between three and five per cent a year." "Recent Developments in Apprentice Training," *Monthly Labor Review* 69:126 (August, 1949). At that rate, A.B.C. could not hope to meet its replacement needs by training apprentices even if its program, based on 1947 employment, were maintained at the maximum possible level.

of these upgraders retained journeyman status in the plant after the war (five of the skilled workers who were interviewed were wartime upgraders) but most of them were reduced to nonskilled jobs. Some wartime upgraders who were reduced to nonskilled work left the plant to secure skilled jobs in other plants where their experience could be passed off as adequate qualification. The presence of a reservoir of workers with some training and experience further limited the opportunities for other non-skilled workers to acquire trade skills. Should openings occur which cannot be filled by fully trained workers, former upgraders are the obvious choice for advancement. Only if there were a substantial increase in the size of the plant, coupled with a shortage of skilled labor greater than the number of available ex-upgraders, could other nonskilled workers hope to be chosen for rapid training.

By June, 1951, employment in the plant had risen because of defense production to about nine thousand and the number of skilled workers had increased to about nine hundred. Such an expansion undoubtedly provided a large number of opportunities both for ex-upgraders and, perhaps, for others, as well as enabling the plant to increase the number of apprentices to sixty. If there had not been such an expansion, unpredictable in 1947 and 1948, there probably would have been no more than a handful of openings each year for which newly trained apprentices and former upgraders would have had priority.

The obvious escape hatch from wage labor on the factory floor is fore-manship, a goal widely pictured as open to those able and ambitious men who are willing to work hard and who display the qualities of initiative and leadership. Even the union lends support to this traditional image, illustrated by the reprinting in the local C.I.O. weekly of a poem by Edgar Guest entitled "Ready for Promotion?" It began:

> There's going to be a vacancy
>   Above you later on,
> Some day you'll find the foreman
>   Or the superintendent gone.
> And are you growing big enough
>   When this shall be the case
> To quit the post you're holding now
>   To step into his place?

Foremanship is popularly envisioned as the lowest rung in the management ladder, the first step toward more responsible, better-paid posts in the corporation.

The advantages of the foreman's position are obvious. He earns considerably more money than wage labor; in 1947 the minimum salary for foremen in all plants of the Corporation was $250 per month, and management policy called for a salary for each foreman that was at least 125% of the average rate of the five highest-paid workers under his supervision. Foremen draw a regular salary free from the uncertainties that plague employees whose earnings depend upon the number of hours they work each week. Foremanship offers the personal satisfaction that comes from increased authority and responsibility, and from higher status both in the factory and in the community. In the factory this new status is symbolized in such things as what one wears to work—shirt and tie, suit trousers, sometimes a vest, instead of denim shirt open at the collar and a pair of work pants. This status is organizationally confirmed by membership in the A.B.C. Executive Club which consists of all members of the management "team." In the community this higher status is visibly demonstrated in one's appearance as one goes to work and in the things that can be bought with increased income.

In this factory of about six thousand workers about 350 men were in supervisory positions. Although workers generally spoke of "foremen" and "supervision" as an undifferentiated group, the supervisory hierarchy led from assistant foreman to foreman, general foreman, and divisional superintendent. Since opportunity for workers simply meant entry to this hierarchy, we need not be concerned with its gradations. In normal times, only ten or twelve openings for workers occur each year as assistant foremen die, retire, quit, or are promoted. "When a fellow gets to be a foreman, he holds it sometimes for twenty-five years," said the personnel manager in an interview. Only during the rapid expansion occasioned by the war did a large number of new openings occur, increasing the size of the supervisory group to about 650. When the plant returned to civilian production, approximately three hundred men were dropped from supervisory positions. About ten per cent of these men, according to the plant's personnel director, took separation pay offered to them by management and struck out in some other field, usually small business. But the remaining ex-foremen constituted a group of experienced men from whom management could, if it wished, recruit supervisory personnel as needed.

Opportunities for promotion to foremanship are in general somewhat greater for skilled workers than for those without skills. The ratio of foremen to skilled workers is higher than the ratio of foremen to nonskilled workers, since skilled departments are usually smaller than other departments in the plant. Not only are there likely to be more supervisory openings for skilled workers, but it is also easier for management to appraise the capabilities of men who possess technical skills and training which may be useful in a supervisory role.

At the time of the research, no formal machinery for selecting foremen existed. (The A.B.C. management has since instituted a formal program for appraising and training prospective foremen.) Foremen would recommend candidates for promotion when an opening occurred. Each candidate would then be carefully considered by the general foreman under whom he would serve and by the superintendent of the division. According to management, the recommendations and the final choice were based upon merit and ability, upon the possession of the necessary technical skills and knowledge, of the personal prerequisites required, and upon the demonstration of competence in the jobs performed in the plant. Here, it appears, is the situation described by the tradition: men must compete for available opportunities by demonstrating their ability, willingness to work, initiative, and drive.

Despite management's undoubted care in choosing foremen—"We take an awfully good look before we make a man a foreman," said the plant's personnel manager—there were no clearly defined criteria of merit to serve as guides to workers' efforts to gain promotion. The only thing of which they could be sure was that they must so impress their foreman that they would be recommended for promotion when a supervisory opening occurred. And while workers were encouraged to believe that their job performance would count, management, according to the personnel manager, has been increasingly choosing workers with considerable formal training. High-school graduation has come to be an important, although not a formal, prerequisite for advancement. Concomitantly management has tended to select as supervisors men who had gone to the nearby state college or men who had been trained at the technical school operated by the Corporation.

Two other criteria over which workers can have little if any control have also entered into the selection of foremen. Since management has tended, according to the personnel manager, to choose workers who are, on the average, in their thirties, the chances of becoming a foreman diminish rapidly as men pass forty. At the same time, however, seniority may play a minor role, although only in some departments. Group leaders, who are given minor supervisory responsibilities and receive a few cents more per hour, are obvious choices for supervision. They may be chosen on the basis of seniority if they possess the necessary skills and leadership attributes. (Since the qualifications for group leaders include such intangibles as the capacity for leadership, however, management has been most successful in challenging the seniority rule in choosing them.) In any event, group leaders are few in number and are largely concentrated in the divisions with skilled workers. There were thirty-four leader classifications among the three-hundred-odd skilled workers, compared with only twelve among the remaining workers, and only one in automotive production where sixty-two per cent of all workers were employed.

Those workers who do become foremen, by and large, have gone about as far as they can go. Despite the claims that "the foreman group is traditionally a middle class into which any able member of the lower class can graduate and from which any able man can graduate into the upper classes,"[6] workers lack the education and training which have come to be major prerequisites for the more responsible, better-paid position.

Yet even with the limited opportunities and the obstacles in the path, foremanship is virtually the only way up for factory workers. There is little likelihood that they can secure advancement by jumping from the factory to white-collar work in the office, the other possible alternative. Occasionally a worker may attract management's attention as someone who might be useful in the personnel department; one such case was mentioned by several union officials, but it was looked upon as something of a freak occurrence. A college graduate who found himself in the factory might be able to transfer to a salaried white-collar job. But workers as a rule possess neither the unusual personal qualifications nor the educational prerequisites for most white-collar jobs.

These facts of jobs, pay, and promotion constitute the objective structure of opportunity in the factory. It is a structure which can hardly be said to live up to the rich promises of American tradition. As we have seen, there are only slim chances of rising into either the skilled "aristocracy of labor" or into the managerial hierarchy. For each one who climbs the ladder there are fifty or a hundred who must remain at roughly the same job level. In these objective circumstances, what prospects do workers see for themselves in the factory? What goals attract their attention and channel their efforts?

Footnotes to Chapter IV

1. See, for example, F. H. Harbison and R. Dubin: *Patterns of Union-Management Relations,* Chicago, Science Research Associates, 1947, p. 77.
2. See N. W. Chamberlain: *The Union Challenge to Management Control,* New York, Harper & Brothers, 1948, pp. 281–282.
3. F. W. Harbison: "Seniority in Mass Production Industries," *J. Political Economy* 48:859 (December, 1940).
4. See H. J. Williams: "Apprentice Training," *American Machinist,* May 22, 1947, pp. 113–128; "Boom in Apprentice Training," *Business Week,* December 6, 1947, pp. 110–113; "Recent Developments in Apprentice Training," *Monthly Labor Review* 69:126–130 (August, 1949).
5. Williams, *op. cit.,* p. 116.
6. Drucker: *Concept of the Corporation,* p. 164.

V

Goals in the Factory: Out of the Ranks

The structure of opportunity in the A.B.C. plant gives most workers little reason to "think of the corporation as a pyramid of opportunities from the bottom toward the top with thousands of chances for advancement" and scant basis for believing that "only capacity limited any worker's chances to grow, to develop his ability to make a greater contribution to the whole and to improve his own position as well." In this plant, with its preponderance of nonskilled jobs, compressed wage scale, seniority rule for individual wage promotions, and few and uncertain opportunities for advancement into the skilled trades or into the ranks of management, there were few men who gave evidence of the high ambition and relentless perseverance sanctioned by tradition.

Among the workers interviewed none spoke of any ambitions in the plant higher than foremanship or, as in one case, an accountant's job in the plant offices. While they all knew of executives who had begun their careers as wage workers—the directors of personnel and of labor relations in the plant were frequently pointed out as examples—the pattern of working one's way up from the ranks was seen as largely a thing of the past. The most significant growth of the A.B.C. plant occurred late in the nineteen-twenties; rising in management was presumably far easier during those years than it has been since. The workers who were interviewed were clearly aware that engineering and management have become so highly selective as to exclude them almost completely.

> For a fellow starting as an hourly worker [said a twenty-four-year-old truck-driver who had only worked in the plant for two years] there isn't much chance of going up there in the company. That's in the past now. In the olden days they used to send out bulletins with pictures of who got promotions and things like that in them all the time. Well, all those fellows started in the factory on hourly wages. But they started in 1910 and 1915 and 1920—twenty-five, thirty, thirty-five years ago. There's not the same chances now. The ones with specialized training get the jobs now. There were three fellows promoted recently, they're right up there, right in the five or six big ones. They're all young fellows, they all have

degrees in engineering. I think the Corporation picks its men now, they don't take them from the ranks.

Any lingering hopes that might survive the knowledge that they lack the prerequisites for conspicuous advancement are likely to be extinguished by the difficulties these workers see in taking the first step off the factory floor into supervision or into some salaried white-collar job.

Salaried positions in the company offices were rarely mentioned even as possible alternatives to work in the factory. Only one of the sixty-two men interviewed expressed interest in and hope for a salaried white-collar job. This one exception had graduated from college in the mid-thirties but had been able to find work only as a W.P.A. supervisor until, with the coming of the war, he had been hired as a timekeeper, at that time a salaried job. When timekeepers voted in 1946 to join the union, their status was changed to that of hourly wage workers. This one ambitious timekeeper had majored in economics in college and was taking a correspondence course in accounting in hope of securing a job in the company's accounting department. In June, 1951, he was still a timekeeper.

The general lack of interest in white-collar office positions and the positive preference expressed by some men for manual work as against "pushing a pencil" or "sitting at a desk" undoubtedly stem in part from the fact that hardly any workers possessed the qualifications of the one hopeful timekeeper. Of the forty-six nonskilled workers for whom data on education are available, twelve had gone no further than grade school and seventeen had not completed high school, a total of roughly two-thirds who had not received the high-school diploma which might be taken as the usual minimum prerequisite for white-collar work.* (Skilled workers, almost by definition, prefer to work with their hands.) Of the remaining seventeen nonskilled workers, several with mechanical interests had taken vocational or technical courses in high school.† Lack of education may, of course, result from the same factors which generate preference for work with one's hands. But even if this is the case, workers who have ended their education early are excluded from alternatives they may some day come to look upon as desirable.

Linked to the lack of education may be the insecurity and self-consciousness of men whose lives have been spent in overalls or work pants and

* In 1940 over eighty per cent of all operatives and a somewhat higher proportion of all laborers in the automotive industry in that group of states of which Autotown's state is one had not completed high school.

† If, as seems likely, the proportion of automobile workers who are high-school graduates increases with the increase in the proportion of the total population who complete high school, the future might find manual workers paying more attention to the possibility of jumping from factory to office.

who have never acquired the social skills which are needed when one is constantly working with people rather than with machines. It is the sort of thing that the man of limited education and social background is likely to feel when he faces "polite society."

Even those whose high-school diplomas might enable them to handle white-collar jobs may see no economic advantage to be gained. In 1947, when hourly wages averaged approximately $1.45, workers were earning a gross weekly income of fifty-eight dollars, an income that undoubtedly compared favorably with what they might earn at the bottom of the white-collar hierarchy. Since by and large these workers did not think in long-range terms,* their present high wages offset the possibility that in the long run white-collar employment might lead to much higher earnings.

Despite the objective importance of foremanship as the initial step forward for factory workers and its sanction by tradition, most of the men interviewed lacked hope for or interest in the possibility of rising into the ranks of supervision. In some cases they even denied its desirability. Of the sixty-two workers interviewed, thirty-one said that they had "never thought of becoming a foreman" or failed to mention foremanship at all in discussing their hopes and plans for their future in the factory. Ten workers reported that they had given up the hopes they had once held of becoming foremen. Fifteen, including four who claimed that they had rejected proffered promotion to supervision, said that they would not want to become foremen.† Only six of the workers interviewed wanted to become foremen and felt that they had a good chance to do so.‡

The lack of interest, hope, and desire was so widespread among the workers interviewed that it must be considered the "normal" reaction to the circumstances in which they found themselves. This generally negative attitude toward foremanship is to be explained primarily as the reaction to the actual limitations on the opportunities available, to the uncertainties stemming from the informal procedures by which foremen were chosen, and to the nature of the foreman's job itself, as these workers see it. Whether men respond to these circumstances by disclaiming interest, by losing hope, or by belittling the goal depends upon such factors as tempera-

---

* See Chapter IX.

† In his study of New Haven workers, E. W. Bakke also found "a rather general lack of enthusiasm for such promotion." *The Unemployed Worker*, New Haven, Yale University Press, 1940, p. 52. In a *Fortune* poll of factory workers in 1947, fifty-eight per cent said that they would not "care particularly" to be foremen. *Fortune*, May, 1947, p. 6.

‡ In the 1947 *Fortune* poll, only twelve per cent thought that they would some day become foremen. *Loc. cit.*

ment, self-evaluation, the idiosyncrasies of past experience, and various other social and psychological characteristics which were not intensively and systematically studied. On the superficial level of skill, age, education, seniority, and the general character of past experience there was little difference among those without interest, those without hope, and those who denied the desirability of the goal.

We have already noted the small number of openings which could be expected to occur each year, the reservoir of wartime foremen who had an obvious priority, the preference for younger men, and the increasing importance of formal education.* That these facts did discourage interest, hope, and desire is evident from the following comments:

> *From a thirty-three-year-old machine-operator with five years of seniority and no interest in foremanship:* There's no chance of getting to be a foreman. Advancement is very slow. There are few who get any place. The ones who were foremen during the war—and there are lots of them around—they'll be the first to go up.

> *From a forty-five-year-old stock-picker with thirteen years of seniority:* I used to hope that I could get on supervision but I'm giving up that idea. I'm getting kind of old—I'm well past forty—and they pick younger fellows and put them on now.

> *From a twenty-seven-year-old line-tender who had graduated from high school but, after seven years in the factory, had given up hope of becoming a foreman:* Foremen are pretty well held down to the people who trained for it, like from [the Corporation's technical school]. When they graduate from there, they're rated to be a supervisor of some sort. It's quite hard to break into foremanship otherwise.

Only one of the thirty-two workers who were over thirty-five years old felt that there was some likelihood of becoming a foreman, while five of the thirty men who were under thirty-five had hopes of doing so. Three of the twenty-two men who had graduated from high school had such hopes, compared with three of the thirty-eight who had not completed high school. (No data were available about education for two men, one without interest, one with vanished hopes.)

It is significant that the objective chances for advancement were better than average for five of the six workers who felt that they were on the path to supervision. The characteristics of these men are given in Table 7. We have already seen that five of the six were under thirty-five years of age and that three were high-school graduates. Four of the six were skilled workers whose chances, as we have pointed out, were better than those of nonskilled workers. One of the nonskilled workers was a group leader in the material-handling division, a position which can be looked upon as a likely prelude to supervision. The one worker who was over thirty-five

---

* See pp. 44–45.

was a toolmaker. Of the three men without high-school diplomas, one was the nonskilled group leader, the two others were skilled. The fact that five of these six belonged to the union suggests that union membership is not looked upon as a handicap in gaining promotion.

Table 7

CHARACTERISTICS OF WORKERS WITH HOPE OF BECOMING FOREMEN

Age	Education	Job	Seniority	Past Experience
29	High school	Toolmaker	1942	Apprentice
31	High school	Die-designer	1934	Line assembler, night courses leading to wartime upgrading
31	Grade school	Machine repair	1935	Line assembler, machine-operator, upgrader
32	High school	Inspector	1937	Line assembler, upgrader, reduced to inspector
34	Some high school	Group leader, material-handling	1935	Laborer in material-handling
46	Grade school	Toolmaker	1934	Apprentice

For three of these workers, the two upgraders and the group leader, their present jobs represented a marked advancement in the factory. Another, the inspector, had been reduced from a wartime skilled classification, but as an inspector he held a job which, as we shall see, was generally defined as much better than the line assignment he had had before the war. These facts suggest the hypothesis that workers are most likely to develop or sustain hope of rising from the ranks if they manage while they are still relatively young to achieve some such advancement as did these four. It is worth noting that only one of the ten workers who had given up hope had gained any significant advancement in the factory. This single exception was a toolmaker who had completed his apprenticeship in 1931; he had suffered from temporary unemployment and the necessity of taking nonskilled jobs until 1938 when he managed to transfer to the toolroom where he could practice his trade. After fifteen years in the factory he had become a group leader. Two other men who had lost hope had once been line-tenders and now held more desirable nonskilled jobs, but both were already in their forties and both had been reduced after the war from the skilled jobs to which they had been upgraded.

By June, 1951, only one of the six men with hope had gained the desired promotion, the toolmaker who had been twenty-nine years old in 1948. It is perhaps significant that this one successful worker had studied engineering for two years at the Corporation's technical school and had transferred to toolmaking when he failed one course, receiving credit for his study and work in engineering in his apprentice training. One of the hopeful six, a die-designer, had left the A.B.C. plant in order to take a job in another city similar to the one he had held. The other four were still at the same jobs.

The second major reason for the lack of interest, hope, and desire lay in the uncertainties of the procedure for selecting foremen. Management insisted that no formal criteria such as age or education mattered if men worked hard and demonstrated outstanding merit and ability. But by exhibiting an obvious preference for younger men with a high-school diploma or with additional training, management belied its own assertions in such a way as to lead some workers to conclude, as we have already seen, that their age or lack of formal education ruled out the possibility of promotion to supervision. By failing on the other hand to spell out the concrete meaning of merit and ability and to establish clear measures of competence and performance, management also left those workers who did not feel that age and education were important prerequisites without a reliable version of what to do in order to strengthen their chances for advancement.

One might, therefore, have expected to hear frequent references to luck as a major element in promotion, for when men can see no clear connection between effort and reward, they "tend to put stress on . . . the workings of Fortune, Chance, Luck."[1] Yet in only one case did a worker express the feeling that "if you were lucky, if you just happened to be in the right place at the right time, you'd get ahead in the shop." Workers were not always able to explain just how men were selected for promotion to supervision, but they knew well enough that little in the plant was left to chance. They could see clearly that their fate in the factory did not rest fundamentally on accidents and unpredictable occurrences, but that it depended upon carefully thought-out decisions of a limited group of men.

The absence of a clearly defined and readily understood machinery for selecting foremen led some workers to assert that they did not know how management chose supervisors. Others gave diverse explanations of how they thought foremen were selected, based on their own experience and observations and on the stories they had heard from others which were part of the frequently inconsistent folklore of the factory.

The admission of ignorance concerning the selection of foremen may be related to workers' attitudes toward the possibility of such advancement in various ways. It may on the one hand help to explain the lack of hope or interest; since they do not know, foremanship remains out of mind or out of reach. On the other hand, this lack of knowledge may merely reflect the lack of interest; the fifty-three-year-old line-tender with only four years of seniority who said that he did not know how foremen were chosen may never have had enough interest to think about it or to try to find out. Or, finally, this confession of ignorance may reflect the uncertainty and confusion that results from failure, as in the case of a forty-five-year-old stock-picker with vanished hopes who remarked bitterly: "I wish I knew how they pick their foremen; I see guys getting promoted, but I don't know why."

When workers tried to explain how foremen were chosen, they agreed only on two general points: that persistent effort, a good performance record, and faithful adherence to company rules, all sanctioned by tradition and encouraged by management as representing evidence of merit and ability, were not in themselves enough to gain promotion; and that whatever a man's other qualifications, he also needed "pull" or "connections" in order to become a foreman.

Workers differed widely, however, in their attitudes toward merit and ability as prerequisites for foremanship, ranging in their views from those who held that such qualities were totally irrelevant* to those who felt that they were necessary but not sufficient and needed to be supplemented by pull. A thirty-year-old machine-operator who had given up his hopes after five years in the factory remarked:

> They say they pick foremen by merit and ability. But they put one guy on supervision on the night shift and then something came up and he couldn't handle it so they sent everybody home until they could get the foreman on the day shift to take care of things. They can't tell me they pick them by merit and ability.

A forty-eight-year-old line-tender with six years of seniority who had also given up his hopes felt that "It's one-third ability and two-thirds pull." And an ambitious and hopeful thirty-one-year-old die-designer commented:

> There was a change in one department over there recently. They picked a fellow to be a supervisor, he's a capable fellow, but I don't know if he's more capable than the other fellows in the department. Maybe the company knew more about all of them than I know, but I think it was just the fact that the superintendent liked him that got him the job.

The general skepticism concerning the efficacy of merit and ability as prerequisites for foremanship stemmed not only from the lack of clear measures of competence, however, but also from the inability to demon-

---

* One union official commented cynically: "If you're any good you can't get promoted because if you do a good job they just keep you on that job. They're afraid they might not get anybody as good as that." That there may occasionally be some basis for this statement was suggested many years ago by R. F. Hoxie: "The employer is loath to take a worker from a task where he is making a high efficiency record." *Scientific Management and Labor*, New York, Appleton, 1914, p. 93.

strate on many jobs such desired personal qualities as initiative, leadership, resourcefulness, and cooperativeness. Even unusual mechanical competence is not easily displayed in standardized jobs which are closely timed and carefully supervised.* Useful technical suggestions, the factory equivalent of the "better mousetrap" of tradition, are rewarded by bonuses; they are not, according to the plant's personnel manager, taken into account in selecting new foremen.

Since promotions in this large and impersonal plant are given by men who are guided by no formal rules, the familiar and frequently repeated slogan, "It's not what you know but who you know" took on particular cogency. Pull and connections were widely looked upon as the major supplements to or alternatives for merit and ability as prerequisites for foremanship, although, it should be noted, this view seemed to be less prevalent among skilled workers whose technical competence, initiative, and leadership could be more readily appraised.

By pull and connections these workers meant two things: the personal interest and support of one's foreman, and ties with someone else in management who might be able to "put in a good word" to facilitate one's advancement. One could bring oneself to the foreman's attention and enlist his support, according to many of these workers, only by using such techniques as "driving the foreman to work every day," "having a smooth tongue when you talk to the foreman," "taking the foreman with you when you go fishing for a weekend," "running around squealing on everybody," or "doing more than your production and then talking to the foreman about how bad everybody else is." One had to "buddy up to the foreman" and "be nice to the foreman" above and beyond the formal requirements of one's job.†

One could only be chosen as a foreman, according to some workers, if one had family connections, or if one had connections by virtue of belonging to the "right" organizations. According to the forty-eight-year-old

---

* A few workers felt that a minimum of error or scrap in production only meant that the foreman did not have to pay any attention to one's work, even though this fact itself, as we shall see later, might be a source of personal satisfaction. On the other hand, bad work would quickly draw the foreman's attention, irate and critical though it might be. The result, however, they felt, was that the foreman knew the less efficient workers but was unacquainted with the better workers.

† Bakke has suggested that the success manual for the modern factory worker will not be entitled "How to stand on your own feet," but "How to get your foot in" or "How to please the boss." Op. cit., p. 87. But the success manual has always devoted a large share of its recommendations to "How to please the boss." The traditional success stories abound with heroes whose advancement was based on some action which pleased the "boss." "How to stand on your own feet" has been the title of the success manual for the small business man; in large organizations advancement has always required the approval of one's superiors. The key question has been how to acquire that approval.

line-tender with no hope left who felt that "It's one-third ability and two-thirds pull": "The biggest share of fellows on supervision have got relatives they're working in. Take a lot of the older ones, they're working in their boys." And a skeptical union committeeman who did not want to be a foreman commented:

> It used to be you had to be a Catholic in order to be a foreman. Now the way it works you have to be a Catholic in one division, in another division you have to be a Mason, and in another an Elk.

Most men, however, did feel that pull alone was not enough to gain promotion to foremanship; one had to be able to do the job in some more or less adequate fashion.

According to a few workers, it was possible to become a foreman without connections if one could acquire some distinction apart from one's job which would elicit favorable attention from management. One worker felt that an active union steward might be chosen as a foreman more readily than an ordinary worker because of management's awareness of his abilities; and a note in the local labor weekly newspaper quoted a worker whose hitchhiking vacation had come in for previous comment as saying: "Keep it up. I want the corporation to know who I am. I want advertising."

None of these varied versions of how foremen were selected, whatever their validity, are likely to sustain or stimulate hope or encourage interest. The rich variety of invidious terms applied to techniques for gaining the personal favor of the foreman, terms such as *bootlicking, brownnosing,* being a *red apple boy* or a *suck pup,* showed the prevalent distaste for such methods of seeking advancement, as over against just doing one's job well. The legacy of preunion labor policies in the automobile industry has probably contributed significantly to the intense condemnation of such techniques of gaining favor. Older workers spoke bitterly of once having to contribute to Christmas gifts for the foreman, of having to mow his lawn or do other chores for him in the days of an overcrowded labor market merely in order to hold a job.

Connections elsewhere in management are difficult to come by. Family ties obviously cannot be manipulated (the factory worker can hardly expect to marry the boss's daughter), and organizational ties which might prove useful cannot be easily developed. Of the twenty-five workers for whom full data on organizational membership are available, two belonged neither to the union nor to any other organization. Eight belonged to the union only, one only to a church group, and one only to an athletic club. Of the remaining thirteen, all union members, ten also belonged to one or more fraternal or veterans' organizations, two belonged to church groups, and one was a Boy Scout troop leader. Advancement may perhaps be facilitated on occasion by club or lodge membership, but this is more likely to be an unanticipated consequence of activity undertaken for other reasons than the result of a consciously planned strategy.* The alternatives are too numerous and the results are too uncertain to permit a systematic campaign to develop connections. Union leadership rarely served as a proving ground for potential foremen, according to the plant's personnel manager, and the opportunities for personal distinction outside the factory which might impress management are few and of doubtful utility.

Workers frequently accounted for their lack of interest or lack of hope by referring to these diverse explanations of how foremen were chosen. For example, a forty-two-year-old repairman in the final assembly division with fourteen years of seniority who had given up hope commented resentfully:

> I don't think I'll ever get to be a foreman because I won't suck the foreman's rear end. There ain't no damn chance of getting on supervision unless you make a damn fool of yourself like that. The superintendent in the X division, I used to work with him on the line, that's how he got there.

And a truck-driver with twelve years of seniority who said that he was not interested in becoming a foreman explained:

> It isn't so much what you know, but it depends on who you know and what lodge you belong to. For instance, I have a friend, he belonged with some other guy who was made a foreman and then he was made a foreman. They say it wasn't that, but—. And the other guy's father-in-law was a general foreman too. A man sees those things and he doesn't figure he's got a chance.

Obviously these explanations may only be rationalizations of the failure to gain advancement or of the lack of interest in a goal sanctioned by tradition. But to the extent that these ideas have a quasi-independent existence as part of the shop folklore, are constantly repeated and reinforced in shop talk, and are transmitted to newcomers or to the children of factory workers who eventually find themselves in the plant, they may well serve to inhibit interest and to stifle hope.

Given the obstacles to advancement to supervision and the uncertainties in the selection process, it is easy to imagine the build-up of verbal objec-

---

* The markedly greater organizational membership in the middle class as compared with the working class, which has been frequently documented, may perhaps be partially explained by the greater economic usefulness of such memberships for men in middle-class occupations.

tions to the seemingly desirable goal of foremanship as a defensive cover-up to blunt one's guilt over not getting ahead or over the failure to sustain the ambition so strongly encouraged by tradition. And one may similarly conceive of the lack of interest in foremanship as psychological protection against the likelihood of failure. Yet it is not unlikely that both the disparagement of foremanship and the lack of interest are in many cases genuine.

The foreman's role itself entails problems and responsibilities which, in the eyes of some workers, counterbalance its advantages. Objective difficulties in the position of the foreman in modern industry have been richly documented in recent years.[2] The development of staff departments (personnel, safety, time-study engineering) in large corporations and the growth of unions have narrowed his authority. The foreman has come to be the transmission belt for orders from above; his job is to enforce rules and carry out policies that originate elsewhere. To perform this job adequately he must secure the active cooperation of his workers; he can no longer rely upon his unchallenged authority. And in attempting to perform this double-barreled task the foreman may find himself caught between pressures from below and pressures from above.

It was this aspect of the foreman's position that workers focussed upon most frequently when denying its desirability. For example, a thirty-two-year-old fender-wrapper in parts and service whose father had been a foreman and who had himself been in the factory for twelve years commented:

> I've thought about being a foreman, but with the grief they've got I'm not sure I would want it. It isn't what it's cracked up to be. The foreman is the middleman. He's caught between the management on the one side and the workers on the other. He's got to try to get along with both of them.

This problem was made particularly acute, it was felt, because of management policies. Some feeling existed that management did not like the foreman to get along too well with his workers. Failure to file an occasional reprimand,* it was claimed, was taken by management as evidence of poor supervision.

Some workers therefore rejected foremanship because they felt that they could not live up to what they asserted was management's definition of the foreman's role. "The foreman is rode [sic!] to get out production," said a machine-operator, "and so he's got to ride his men. I couldn't do that." "I've been offered a foreman's job," said a welder in his mid-thirties who

---

* In the A.B.C. plant, offenses against company regulations which were not serious enough to warrant discharge or temporary suspension were noted by a written reprimand which was filed in the employee's personnel record.

was a union committeeman, "but I'll never take it. I don't feel I could carry through company policy to the fellows and still be the individual I want to be." It is possible, of course, that a strong identification with the union might stimulate this feeling.

If the foreman tries to avoid censure from above and to win approval from his superiors by rigidly enforcing company rules and by following company policies closely, he is likely to antagonize his workers, who can easily harass him and make his job more difficult, as men knew from their own experience. One union committeeman told of a case in which a foreman had fired a worker who had violated an unpopular company rule.

> I told the foreman that the men were ready to swear that he had cursed at the fellow and abused him until he got mad and did something the foreman fired him for. The foreman had already sent the firing slip to the Personnel Department, but he backed down anyway. Then he found himself on management's hot spot because he couldn't explain what happened.

Since the foreman is held responsible for production in his department, workers can get back at him by making "accidents" happen that would slow up output. While a competent foreman undoubtedly avoids these dangers and mediates successfully between workers and higher management, men without considerable confidence in their ability to handle these problems may view them as sufficient reason for rejecting the desirability of foremanship.

From the security of their collective situation in the factory, these men frequently look critically at the foreman's exposure to the authority of higher management. Foremen were frequently described as the persons on whom their superiors could "take out their troubles," as the scapegoats for the errors of their superiors and as subject to their whims. A truck-driver who said that he would not want to be a foreman explained:

> There's too much grief in the foreman's job. There's one fellow I know who took the job, he was on it for two days. They didn't like something he was doing so they came down and really laid it into him. So he told them to keep the job. When the superintendent starts yelling at the foreman, he just has to say "yes, yes, yes," be a regular "yes-man." And the language they use, like one fellow used to always call the foreman "Stupid," so the men just called him "Stupe."

Without a union to protect him (attempts to organize a foreman's union in the plant in 1945 and 1946 were abortive), the foreman appears to these workers to occupy an insecure as well as difficult position, open to the potential tyranny of arbitrary authority.

All these liabilities may appear even more significant to the skilled worker whose objective chances of becoming a foreman are better than those of the nonskilled worker. Unless he is promoted to a supervisory position in his own department where he would be directing the work of other skilled craftsmen, he must break with his trade and surrender the satisfactions that go with performance at a high level of skill. Because skilled workers earn considerably more than nonskilled workers, the increase in earnings gained by promotion to supervision of nonskilled labor is not likely to be very great. Even the advantages of foremanship in his own department may not compensate for its uncertainties and difficulties, particularly since he normally earns premium wages doing interesting work in a department which is usually small and stable enough to permit the development of satisfying social relationships with his fellows.

For some workers, both skilled and nonskilled, the fact of responsibility itself makes foremanship appear undesirable. "I've never thought about being a foreman," said a machine-operator in his fifties who had been in the plant for twelve years. "There's too much responsibility." This avoidance of responsibility may mean lack of confidence in one's ability to do the job. (It has been shown from public-opinion data that lower-class persons frequently do tend to lack self-confidence.)[3] Or it may mean that one is unwilling to assume the obligations of authority, the burden of making decisions, and the risks of accountability for the performance of others. We know little of the personality characteristics which distinguish those who welcome responsibility from those who fear it, or of the conditions under which men accept or reject responsibility, but there is some evidence that working-class men are particularly likely to avoid it.[4]

In the modern mass-production plant, nonskilled workers have little opportunity to learn how to handle responsibility; carefully engineered and closely timed jobs give little room for the exercise of discretion or the making of significant decisions. Workers at the bottom of the corporate hierarchy learn to combat authority or to accept it, not how to exercise it. A thirty-one-year-old truck-driver who had gone to work on the assembly line at the age of eighteen and had held various other nonskilled jobs commented:

> I've never thought about the possibility of getting to be a foreman. I don't think they'd give it to anybody anyway without some sort of special training. We're not trained for leadership. We sometimes kid around—"you're trying for a foreman's job"—but we're not trained to manage men. We're trained to work together and we just do the best we can.

Lacking experience and the *savoir-faire* that comes from experience, perhaps uncertain of their ability to handle the problems they would face as foremen, workers show no interest in the possibility of foremanship or go on to deny its desirability.

The loss of hope, the lack of interest, and the disparagement of foremanship must thus be seen, as we have suggested, as "normal" responses to the limited opportunities available, to the uncertainties of the procedure by which foremen were chosen, and to the very nature of the foreman's role. But they must also, in a few instances, be related to other factors.

Some men who are securely settled in familiar and satisfying job routines may reject foremanship as they would reject any change. For example, a thirty-five-year-old toolmaker who had been in the plant for seventeen years remarked, in answer to a question about his attitude toward the possibility of foremanship: "I'd rather stay in the plant where I know the work than have to break into something new." This resistance to change is undoubtedly related to the same circumstances that lead men to avoid responsibility —the uncertainty in the face of new problems, the lack of experience, and the absence of self-confidence. In this case, as among skilled workers generally, resistance to change was supported by the positive satisfactions available in the current job.

In a few instances, men were so deeply committed in their aspirations to a business or a farm of their own, or to some other out-of-the-shop goal, that the possibility of foremanship hardly seemed to enter their thoughts. A twenty-year-old unmarried machine-operator, for example, was not interested in foremanship because he was planning to start college at the beginning of the next academic year; work in the factory had from the first been defined as temporary. (It is worth noting that this young man's father was not a factory worker but the owner of a small business.) In most cases, however, in which single-minded dedication to some out-of-the-shop goal seemingly precludes any interest in foremanship, the limited opportunities in the factory may actually play an important role in determining their ambitions. But we can only appraise this hypothesis after we have examined the other alternatives which are theoretically within the reach of these workers, both in the factory and beyond its walls.

Footnotes to Chapter V

1. R. K. Merton: *Social Theory and Social Structure*, Glencoe, Illinois, The Free Press, 1949, p. 138.
2. The efforts of foremen to unionize during and after World War II precipitated a vast literature on the position and problems of supervisory employees. Of the wide variety of available material, see W. F. Whyte and B. Gardner: "The Man in the Middle," *Applied Anthropology* (now *Human Organization*) 4:1–28 (Spring, 1945); F. J. Roethlisberger: "The Foreman: Master and Victim of Doubletalk," *Harvard Business Review* 23:283–298 (Spring, 1945); S. Slichter, R. D. Calkins, W. H. Spohn: "The Changing Position of the Foreman in American Industry," *Advanced Management* 10:155–161 (December, 1945).

3. G. Knupfer: "Portrait of the Underdog," *Public Opinion Quarterly* 7:698–710 (Spring, 1947).
4. See for example A. Davis: "The Motivation of Underprivileged Workers," in W. F. Whyte, Ed. *Industry and Society*, New York, McGraw-Hill Book Company, Inc., 1946, pp. 84–106. Although Davis was concerned primarily with Negro workers, his findings have broader applicability.

VI

Goals in the Factory: On the Level of Wage Labor

With foremanship offering little promise to most workers and with salaried white-collar jobs virtually out of reach, most men must confine their aspirations in the factory to alternatives on the level of wage labor. According to one automobile industry economist, the tradition of opportunity is relevant even on the level of factory labor because of "constant upgrading of individuals . . . limited only by [their] capacity and willingness."[1] But we have seen already that the objective structure of opportunity in the factory provided little chance for upgrading and higher wages. Because skilled work requires formal apprenticeship or on-the-job training that is not easily available to most workers, there is a deep gulf between skilled and nonskilled jobs. The wage scale for the mass of nonskilled jobs, with their limited demands on workers, is highly compressed. And since advancement within this compressed wage structure is usually governed by seniority, there is little room for individual effort, despite the maxims of the tradition of opportunity.

In this chapter we shall examine the kinds of goals pursued by workers in this context of routinized work and limited wage differentials. Do nonskilled workers focus their aspirations on skilled jobs despite the difficulties in their way? To what extent do they center their hopes for advancement on promotion via seniority? Are there other goals in the factory which are not defined by the tradition of opportunity or based upon its values?

Thirty-seven of the forty-seven nonskilled workers interviewed evinced no active interest in skilled work, even though they recognized its desirability not only in terms of wages and steady employment, but also of the work gratifications, prestige, and respect it provided. When asked directly if they had any interest in skilled work or if they had ever thought of trying to acquire trade skills, they either simply said "No" or observed, usually without signs of disappointment or frustration, that skilled work was out of reach and therefore not to be entertained as a goal.

That ten of the forty-seven wanted skilled jobs does not mean, however, that hope and desire, encouraged by the cultural admonition to persevere, had survived despite obstacles in their path. Since eight of the ten were wartime upgraders who had had some experience at part of a skilled job, there was some objective basis for their interest. Yet only two of these eight were sanguine about their chances. As they all knew, management preferred to hire fully qualified journeymen with formal apprentice training or with many years of all-around experience, rather than recall upgraders who had usually learned only part of a skilled trade. Under the union contract former upgraders possessed no legal rights to openings in the skilled trades. Only if the need were so great that skilled tasks could be broken down into their constituent specialties as they had been during the war, or if not enough fully qualified journeymen to meet plant needs could be found, might most upgraders hope to be recalled. During 1946, 1947, and 1948, there seemed little likelihood that such a demand for skilled labor would develop.

There was much discussion during this period, particularly in union circles, of a proposal to offer abbreviated apprentice training to former upgraders who would be given appropriate credit for their wartime experience. All eight former upgraders interviewed rejected the very idea of this proposal, even before it could gain any formal status. Seven had one or more children, the eighth a chronically ill wife. None could have managed easily, if at all, if their wages were cut to the rates paid apprentices. All were in their thirties or forties; none relished the thought of occupying a status in the plant which was normally associated with teen-agers and men in their early twenties, even if it were temporary.

The two workers who had not been upgraders had applied for admission to the toolmaker apprentice program. Both were veterans who could expect federal assistance while securing job training. One was a twenty-four-year-old unmarried machine-operator who had not graduated from high school, but had requested that the education requirement be waived because of his war service. The other was a thirty-two-year-old inspector with several children who hoped that his age would be overlooked because of his military service. Both applications were subsequently rejected.

In June, 1951, despite the plant expansion that had come with the defense program, only one of the ten workers actively interested in skilled work, a former upgrader-electrician, held a skilled job. The other nine still held nonskilled jobs in the factory.

Only four of the forty-seven nonskilled workers had defined their goals in terms of the better-paying next job in their department or division which might come their way on the basis of seniority. A stock-picker in parts and service earning $1.35 per hour hoped to become a clerk at $1.38 per hour; two line assemblers earning $1.44 wanted to become line repairmen at three cents more per hour; and a machine-operator earning $1.44 hoped to become a machine-setter at $1.47. The remaining nonskilled workers either professed no job goals at all in the factory (except for the ten interested in skilled work and one with hope of foremanship), or had focussed their attention upon alternatives which did not offer higher wages.

That so few workers had defined their goals in terms of the better-paying next job does not mean that most men were not concerned with wages and earnings. Workers who say, as did one, "When you bring home the check and the wife says it meets expenses, then you're satisfied," cannot remain unconcerned about wages and earnings. But this interest showed itself in various ways, in the emphasis upon general wage increases, in the intensity with which workers asserted their rights to better-paying jobs assigned on the basis of seniority, in their interest in a steady job. It is a commonplace that the union can always count on strong support from its members when it seeks to gain a general wage increase. When a better-paying job which would normally be filled on the basis of seniority becomes available, the worker with the longest seniority in the appropriate occupational group is ready to file a grievance immediately if his claim is bypassed. Steady jobs, as we shall see, were valued in large part because in long-range terms they were likely to provide a higher income than better-paid but less regular assignments.

That goals did not follow the formal wage hierarchy among nonskilled jobs does suggest, however, that workers had made a more or less realistic appraisal of the alternatives open to them. We have already examined the compressed wage scale which sets narrow limits on the possibility of promotion to better-paying jobs.* Even the small promotions possible within this wage structure might be delayed for a long period of time because of the priority of workers with long seniority. In July, 1947, a third of all workers in the plant had been there for less than two years. This group could expect that those jobs which paid an additional few cents per hour would go to men who had been there for a longer period of time, although the wage range was so narrow than even many of the thirty-seven per cent of the work force with ten years of seniority or more might not be able to secure better-paying assignments.

Workers were usually aware of these facts. "You can be there for years and never get any place," complained a machine-operator with twelve years of service. "I've been here for twenty years," said an inspector sadly, "and

---

* See pp. 37–39.

if I came in tomorrow, I'd make just as much money." "You've got to be here for five or six years at least," said a line-tender with three years of seniority, "before you can expect to get a better job." With only small wage increases possible via promotion, and with a long wait before even these openings occur, workers are not likely to give much thought to the possibility of securing a better-paying job which is inherent in the formal seniority rule.

Such goals as nonskilled workers did pursue in the factory tended to follow an informal hierarchy of desirability instead of the formal structure of advancement. Workers ranked the various kinds of nonskilled jobs in an order of preference which roughly followed divisional and departmental lines but which largely ignored the possibilities of promotion to better-paying jobs within divisions and departments.*

At the bottom of the hierarchy was a small number of unskilled custodial jobs—sweepers, janitors, elevator-operators—not usually assigned to any divisions. These jobs were widely looked upon as reserved for older men who should have retired, but could not afford to, for men who were physically incapable of hard, continuous effort, but were nevertheless retained because of their long seniority. They were the most poorly paid tasks in the plant, carrying wage rates in 1947 of $1.19 to $1.29 per hour. No workers in these classifications were interviewed and no evidence is available as to their actual age distribution, but they were usually characterized by the workers interviewed and by union officials as "old men who couldn't do a real day's work." Prior to the recent introduction of a Corporation pension plan whose impact on workers' attitudes has yet to be assessed, older men who held such jobs provided a daily reminder of what could happen if one grew old in the factory and, as we shall see,† acted as a stimulus to the desire to leave.

Assembly-line work constitutes, for all practical purposes, what may be considered the real bottom of the nonskilled hierarchy of desirability, with machine operation ranking slightly higher. The final assembly departments of the final assembly and axle division were almost completely line work; the axle plant consisted of both line and machine work. The motor division was also divided between line and machine jobs. The paint shop in the sheet-metal and paint division was primarily line work, while the press room and other departments of this division were almost entirely machine operation.

Ranking above these production jobs on the line and at the machine were a variety of other production jobs scattered through the three auto-

---

* For a description of the organization and structure of the plant, see pp. 35-36.

† See p. 84.

motive production divisions: bench assembly, repair work, die- and machine-setting, utility and relief assignments.

At the top of the order of preference were off-production jobs. In some contexts, workers included skilled work in this group, but they usually meant by off-production work jobs in inspection, material-handling, and parts and service, and the nonskilled jobs in the maintenance division.

One can therefore conceive of this hierarchy of desirability, as did most workers, in terms of two overlapping, interrelated sets of categories, as kinds of jobs or as segments of the plant. The relationships between these alternative sets of categories is indicated in the following parallel listing.

Type of Work	Plant Department or Division
Unskilled custodial work	No plant segment
Assembly line	Final assembly
	Paint shop
	Axle plant
	Motor division
Machine operation	Sheet metal (press room)
Miscellaneous production	Chiefly in automotive production
Off-production	Inspection
	Parts and service
	Material-handling
	Shipping
	Material control
	Maintenance (nonskilled)

Nonskilled workers usually phrased their job aims in the factory in terms of the kinds of jobs or the segments of the plant included in the hierarchy of desirability. Several line assemblers wanted to "get off the line," any other alternative being acceptable. Another line assembler was seeking a job in material-handling, a machine-operator wanted to "get into shipping," a line repairman wanted to "get off production." Several line assemblers and machine-operators wanted one or another of the more desirable production jobs—repair work, machine setup, utility work. Only one worker was interested in a job that ranked lower in the hierarchy, and two were seeking jobs on the same level as their current jobs. One of the latter two was the stock-picker who aspired to the better-paying clerk's job in his division.

The values of the tradition of opportunity played only a small role in determining the structure of this informal hierarchy of desirability. Moving up in the hierarchy coincided with earning higher hourly wages only in the case of a few of the miscellaneous production jobs. Indeed, some jobs in off-production divisions ranked high in the order of preference despite the fact that they carried lower-than-average wage rates. And none of the workers interviewed considered alternatives in the plant in terms of their promise for the future. In this they were more realistic than one writer on occupations in the automobile industry who has asserted that the path to the top begins more frequently with assembly-line work than with any other job.[2] He justifies this claim on the grounds that the worker may there learn productive techniques used throughout many branches of an industry which constantly draws its executives from the ranks. But there is little to be learned on the assembly line that may be of use in an executive position or, for that matter, in most other nonskilled jobs in the factory. And we have already seen the gap between management and labor in the industry.

The values which played the greatest part in determining the order of preference among nonskilled jobs were regularity of employment and the relative absence of physical and psychological strain. These values stem primarily from the nature of work in an automobile factory rather than from the tradition of opportunity.

With their experience of regular seasonal layoffs and otherwise erratic employment, automobile workers have translated the traditional emphasis upon advancement to better-paying jobs into a concern with steady work. They have come to look at wages not only in terms of hourly rates, but also with an eye to how much one can earn over an extended period of time. In the long run, they feel, a steady job will provide a better income than an irregular job that pays higher hourly rates. "I can make about two thousand dollars a year on this job and I don't think the guys on the line can make that much even if they are making six cents an hour more," said a stock-picker in parts and service earning $1.35 per hour who had been transferred at his own request from an assembly-line job that brought $1.41 per hour. "I've got the best job in the shop," boasted a yard-maintenance man. "I work fifty-two weeks a year. I don't get paid as much but at the end of the year I'm better off than the guys on production."

Concern with temporary idleness and short workweeks was particularly strong during the period when most of the data were secured because of the dislocations which had accompanied the shift back to civilian production after the war. Shortages of materials and interruptions in the delivery of parts had resulted in frequent short workweeks and occasional layoffs of a few days' duration. The problems created by this irregular employment had been made more pressing by the sudden increase in prices which followed the elimination of price controls in the summer of 1946. (From March, 1946 to December, 1946 the cost of living in Autotown rose about seventeen per cent.) When these men were asked their chief worry, their usual answer was "keeping up with the high cost of living." The financial difficulties created by the drop in take-home pay that had followed the elimination of extended overtime after the war had been aggravated shortly afterward by a long strike which had depleted savings and returned many workers to the pay-day-to-pay-day domestic economy which had prevailed before the war.

Those types of jobs and those divisions which provided the steadiest employment were therefore particularly desirable, even if some of them paid lower hourly rates. Conversely, those most subject to temporary layoffs and short workweeks were least desirable. The ranking of jobs and divisions according to this criterion corresponded to a large extent with the hierarchy of desirability. Line assembly, particularly in the final assembly division, was the most erratic and off-production jobs were the most regular. Machine operation and other production work were equally steady, but neither was as regular as off-production assignments or as irregular as line assembly.

By divisions, axle and final assembly were least desirable, although jobs in the axle plant were somewhat better than those on the final line. The motor and crankshaft and sheet-metal and paint divisions were roughly the same, though with occasional differences from department to department. "When I hired in," said a machine-operator in the motor division with less than a year's seniority, "I had a choice of three jobs, in final assembly, the motor plant, and sheet metal. So I asked what was the steadiest and they told me the motor plant or sheet metal." Most desirable were the inspection, material-handling, parts and service, and maintenance divisions.

When the plant halted operations early in 1947 in order to take inventory, employees in final assembly (except for a few with long seniority) were laid off for two weeks while workers elsewhere in the factory were laid off for only one week. During the period of postwar dislocation, workers in final assembly and in parts of the sheet-metal and paint division averaged only about thirty-five hours of work per week. Workers in other production divisions and departments suffered some short workweeks, although not as frequently as final assembly and the affected departments of the sheet-metal and paint division. Off-production workers enjoyed fairly regular forty-hour workweeks during this period.

These variations in the regularity of employment stem from the very nature of automobile production. Line assembly depends upon the constant flow of parts and materials from many sources; a break in the flow from any source can mean a momentary halt of operations—or a long layoff. Final assembly, usually identified by workers as "first laid off and last called back," is dependent upon the entire array of antecedent steps in production and is therefore most susceptible to interruption. Since machine operation does not usually depend upon as many antecedent steps, it is less likely to be affected immediately by temporary difficulties. The circumstances which meant short workweeks for machine-operators in the sheet-metal and paint division during 1946 and 1947 were due, as most workers knew, to the postwar steel shortage which could not be expected to last indefinitely. (The steel shortage was a recurrent topic in the Autotown newspaper and the union weekly during this period.)

Despite their varied character, the miscellaneous production jobs offered steadier employment than line assembly, but were no steadier than machine operation. Those who were working in assembly-line departments, line repairmen, for example, might expect to work slightly longer than assemblers, but no more regularly than other production workers elsewhere. Those working with machine-operators, die-setters, or utility men, for example, could expect their jobs to be about as regular, or irregular, as others in their departments.

Off-production jobs, although lumped together as more regular, on the whole, than production tasks, actually differ widely. The further removed from current production, the less likely are they to be afflicted with short workweeks or temporary layoffs. Inspectors, who are usually tied to the flow of production, can only expect to work for a few extra hours if line-tenders or machine-operators are sent home early or laid off for a few days. Some workers in material-handling are similarly tied to current production. Those in shipping, on the other hand, together with those in parts and service, are more fortunate since their work normally continues for some time after a stoppage in production departments. They can normally expect to work regular hours without layoffs unless there is a major production stoppage. And many maintenance workers are needed all the time, whether the plant is operating or not.

Beyond the linked values of more money and steady work, there was little that was positive in workers' desires in the factory. They tended to state the values which they applied in appraising job alternatives in negative and defensive terms; most workers approached work in this large, mechanized factory with few illusions and with limited demands.

The very nature of most jobs on the level of nonskilled labor focusses workers' attention on the avoidance of strain, discomfort, and inconvenience. If these men had ever hoped for work which would engage their interests and abilities, they were soon forced, in most instances, to give up such desires.* In the words of one machine-operator who had just returned to the factory after an unsuccessful try at small business:

> I've always heard of those jobs. Like in school I had an economics teacher who first told me that a person has a good job if you can make it your recreation, that's the job for you. Maybe lots of people do have jobs like that, but most people have to work and some jobs are just disagreeable. You understand, if you get a job that you're interested in, when you work you don't pay attention to the time, you don't wait for the whistle to blow to go home, you're all wrapped up in it and don't pay attention to other things. *I don't know one single job like that.*

Nonskilled workers can only choose among jobs which are easier or harder, among jobs which vary in how tightly they tie the worker to one spot and in how completely they determine the speed and tempo at which one must work.

Men wanted work which was "not too hard," "not too heavy," "not too dirty," and "not too noisy." They sought to avoid jobs in which "you can't take a smoke when you want to," or "you can't go to the toilet when you have to but have to wait for the relief man." They did not like jobs in which "you got to keep your hands in oil and grease all day" or "where you get your hands full of steel splinters." The issue here is not laziness, an aversion to work. One could see this in the persistent activity around workers' homes as men tended their gardens, painted their houses, worked on their cars. Indeed, a frequent complaint was that the fatigue after a day on the line or at a machine is so great that one has little energy left for other things one wishes to do.

Without dissent, assembly-line work was looked upon as the most exacting and most strenuous. Its coerced rhythms, the inability to pause at will for a moment's rest, and the need for undeviating attention to simple routines made it work to be avoided if possible and to escape from if necessary.† So demanding is the line that one worker, echoing others, com-

---

* Bakke reports that among the workers he studied in New Haven, "Time and again men said they had started out with big ideas about the dignity of labor and tried to get a 'big kick' out of work itself. It soon wore out and work became a routine to be faced if they wanted to avoid pain and get some comfort out of life." *The Unemployed Worker,* p. 15.

† In spite of the symbolic importance of the assembly line as the epitome of mass-production technology and its concrete significance in the number of workers involved (the Bureau of Labor Statistics' 1950 study of wages in the automobile industry classified fifty thousand workers as "conveyor assemblers"), there has been relatively little objective analysis of assembly-line work. Apart from the valuable discussion by Georges Friedmann, *Ou Va le Travail Humain?* Paris, Gallimard, 1950, pp. 135–142, 225–246, the few articles cited by him, a recently published study by C. R. Walker and R. Guest, *The Man on the Assembly Line,* Cambridge, Harvard University Press, 1952, most of whose findings coincide with those reported here, and some impressionistic reports, there is little material available.

plained: "You get the feeling, everybody gets the feeling, whenever the line jerks everybody is wishing, 'break down, baby.'" But simultaneously workers fear the breakdown they desire. One machine-operator who had spent several years on the assembly line stated this ambivalence explicitly:

> A fellow's always hoping something happens. It's natural on the line. [His wife interrupted: "Just so you're not sent home."] That's right. You don't want it to break down so you get sent home but you want it to stop for a little while and give you a chance to stop for a minute. But you don't want to be sent home because you need the money. You always need the money.

All but two of the line-tenders interviewed hoped to secure some other kind of job in the plant; one was looking toward a career in the union hierarchy and was not much concerned about his current job and the other wanted to leave the factory completely.

Because of its physical and psychological demands, none of the men who had worked on the line in the past would have willingly returned to it. "I'd quit before I'd go back on the line," a repairman with fifteen years of seniority said heatedly. While his seniority would probably keep him from quitting even if it were necessary to go back on the line, his comment indicates the intensity of his feelings. And the persistent overtones of past experience on the line could be seen in workers' attitudes toward their present jobs. An ex-line-worker in parts and service commented:

> I used to work on the chassis line. When I used to get home my hands would go like that. [He held his hands over the edge of the couch on which he was sitting and let them shake helplessly. His wife added: "That's right. He used to be all worn out."] When I worked on the line I felt so bad that when I came home I couldn't do anything. Where I am now I don't have to work so hard and I feel a lot better.

Another man in parts and service who had been on the line for ten of the thirteen years he had been in the plant remarked:

> Now that I'm off the line I don't know how I stood it for ten years. But where I am now I like it. You're not on the same job all the time, and if you want to go missing for a while you can without a foreman running down on you and telling you to get back to work.

Work at a machine may be just as repetitive, require as few motions and as little thought as line assembly, but men prefer it because it does not keep them tied as tightly to their tasks.* "I can stop occasionally when I want to," said a machine-operator. "I couldn't do that when I was on the line."

---

* In a recent English investigation it was found that workers at a conveyor belt were more likely to be dissatisfied than men doing other kinds of routine production jobs. J. Walker and R. Marriott: "A Study of Some Attitudes to Factory Work," *Occupational Psychology* 25:180–191 (July, 1951).

Production standards for a particular machine may be disliked and felt to be excessive, but the machine-operator need only approximate his production quota each day. The line-tender must do all the work that the endless belt brings before him. There is no externally controlled compulsion to maintain a steady work tempo on a machine; it can be stopped for a few minutes to smoke a cigarette or go to the toilet. But the tempo of work on the line is set by the speed at which the conveyor is moving, and the assembler cannot leave his post until replaced by the relief man.

Many of the other production jobs are roughly equivalent to machine operation in the demands they make of workers, but a few provide somewhat greater freedom of movement and flexibility of tempo, as well as variety of task. Line repairmen, for example, have no set job quotas to meet. There may be a steady flow of work during the day; alternatively, an hour may go by with little to do, followed by a period of intense effort as a large number of "cripples" (imperfectly assembled units requiring repairs) come down the line. In a routinized job world, this very irregularity becomes attractive. And line repairmen have the further advantage of some degree of freedom to move up and down the line as they work. This physical mobility also permits a range and variety of social relationships not available to workers who must remain in one place.

Off-production jobs provide the greatest degree of freedom and movement of all nonskilled work. They do not usually tie workers to fixed positions or require the constant repetition of a limited series of movements. Men in parts and service and in material-handling perform simple though unstandardized tasks such as packing parts for shipment, unloading materials, operating power trucks, or looking after a tool crib. Some inspectors, it is true, only operate machines which test finished parts, but others do their work by listening to the motor, making visual or tactile examination of parts, or by manipulating various kinds of gauges. For many off-production tasks no fixed quantitative standards of performance exist against which foremen can measure the efforts of their workers, though they must obviously maintain some standards of efficiency. "That's the advantage of a job off production," said a truck-driver. "There's no set amount of work you have to do. You aren't pushed or crowded like on production."

Workers' concern with the physical and psychological demands of jobs in the factory include an urgent preoccupation with the character of supervision. As a great deal of recent research has indicated,[3] and as our data also demonstrate, the quality of supervision is a major factor in men's attitudes toward their jobs. In a large, necessarily impersonal industrial organization, the foreman can play a significant role with respect to workers' self-esteem.

"A good foreman," explained a press-operator, "makes you feel like somebody, not just like another machine." And a milling-machine-operator complained resentfully: "The trouble is that the foreman just thinks that a man is a piece of machinery and that he can do what he likes without giving a fellow the kind of consideration he ought to get." While men recognized that a considerate and understanding foreman could turn up anywhere, even in final assembly, and that a nagging, crochety, authoritarian foreman might be found in the departments with the best jobs, there was a widespread feeling that off-production jobs were more likely to be blessed with good supervision than were those in production divisions.

This feeling came not from any apparent superiority in the quality of foremen in off-production departments, but from differences in the character of work assignments and the resulting differences in the responsibilities of supervision. In production departments, foremen are chiefly concerned with seeing that workers maintain standards which are set on the basis of systematic job analysis. The line foreman can see whether work is coming through that meets inspection standards. Quantity is determined by the speed of the line. The supervisor of machine operators has a constant record of the volume of output from each machine with which to appraise workers' efforts and efficiency. Failure to meet job standards will quickly invite criticism and possibly threats or sanctions from the foreman. But in off-production jobs, as we have seen, the foreman does not usually have such sharply defined standards against which to check performance. He assigns the work to be done, and as long as it is completed adequately in what seems to be a reasonable time, workers need not fear supervisory criticism. And some off-production assignments, for example, trucking parts from one building to another, even take the worker away from the possibility of direct surveillance. It therefore appears to workers that off-production jobs are not as closely or as rigidly supervised as those in other divisions. The absence of supervision is itself something to be valued, a fact also noted in other studies.[4] "A man likes to be left alone," said a welder, "and not bothered, trusted to do his job without anybody standing over him. It makes a man feel more important that way."

Most workers accepted these values and the validity of the hierarchy based upon them, but here and there one found an individual worker for whom some personal value or some idiosyncratic desire had assumed such overriding significance that other considerations were irrelevant or relatively unimportant. For example, the one worker whose goal was a job that ranked lower in the hierarchy than the one he held was a twenty-four-year-old crankshaft inspector who wanted to transfer to the department in which his father was working, even though this would have meant accepting a machine job.* This one case also suggests the importance workers may assign to satisfying social relations on the job,[5] but the nature of their relationships with co-workers is more likely to hold men to jobs or stimulate the desire for change than it is to lead them to focus their attention and interest on some particular kind of work or some specific assignment elsewhere in the factory. Workers can hardly know in advance the nature of the work group they might find in some other department in the plant.

One of the workers who was interested in a job on the same level of the hierarchy as his current job was a machine-operator who was seeking a similar assignment in an addition to the plant then being built. He wanted to "take a crack at one of those big new machines" being installed in this addition. It seems a plausible hypothesis that this worker was actively searching for more of the ego-enhancement which men may secure from the operation of large, complex machines. In this intensive pursuit he was perhaps atypical, but it is possible that one of the less obvious factors which minimize dissatisfaction with the routine tasks of modern industry is the sense of personal power that workers derive from their ability to control the operations, in however routine a fashion, of giant machines which dwarf their operators.

Opportunities for movement from level to level in the hierarchy of desirability depend upon the rate of labor turnover, plant expansion, and the policies which govern management's utilization of manpower. When the number of workers in the plant remains relatively stable, as it did in 1946 and 1947, opportunities for upward movement depend almost entirely upon the extent and nature of labor turnover. Only as openings occur in the higher levels of the hierarchy can workers with less desirable jobs hope to improve their status.

Turnover data for the plant for August and September, 1946 show that 359 workers left the plant in August and 405 in September. Almost all left voluntarily and management tried to replace most of them. As might be expected, however, turnover was proportionately greater among workers with less desirable jobs than among those with more desirable jobs. Five per cent of A.B.C. workers were in inspection, but only 2.5% of those who left during these two months were inspectors. Similarly, only 4.5% of those who left were in the relatively desirable material-handling division in which nine per cent of all workers were employed. The greatest turnover in all auto-

---

* One other exception to goals which followed the hierarchy of desirability was found in the case of a line-tender who had earlier been transferred from a machine job at his own request. "I had the dirtiest and worst job in the press room," he explained. "My hands were all cut up and they were in grease all the time. It was just so bad I asked for a transfer, and when they told me that all that was open was on the line, I took it."

mobile plants in the city during this period, according to union officials and interviewers in the local offices of the United States Employment Service, was among assembly-line workers.

Since turnover during this period was higher than usual, the number of desirable openings to be filled each month would typically be smaller than these data suggest.* If these proportions hold for periods of average turnover, there would be each month seven or eight job openings in inspection and thirteen or fourteen in material-handling, a total of about twenty-two jobs each month open to approximately 3,600 workers in automotive-production divisions. If these were well-paid jobs, workers already in these off-production divisions would have preference because of seniority within their occupational group or division.

Plant expansion may create new opportunities for movement in the non-skilled hierarchy in addition to those made available by labor turnover. During 1948 and 1949, for example (after the field work for the study was completed), an entirely new division for manufacturing motors was added to the plant to supplement existing facilities. So extraordinarily mechanized was this new division, even by automobile-industry standards, that it required a work force with a high proportion of inspectors and maintenance workers. One machine, for example, was eighty-six feet long, possessed more than ninety cutting tools, and handled seventeen engine blocks simultaneously with each block moving automatically through the entire series of operations. By the beginning of 1949 more than three hundred new multi-purpose automatic machines had already been installed. But, it should be noted, the opportunities created by plant expansion in this case are not necessarily typical of the results of expansion. Adding new facilities may also mean merely an increase in assembly-line or machine tasks, even though there would almost always be at least a few desirable new jobs as well.

The extent to which labor turnover and plant expansion offer opportunity to secure more desirable jobs to workers already in the factory depends upon the policies followed by management in filling job vacancies. If, for example, management fills all desirable openings with newly hired employees, then neither turnover nor expansion can mean opportunity to men already in the plant. If, on the other hand, management policies establish a clear line of movement from assembly line to desirable off-production jobs, then

---

* By applying the turnover rate for Autotown's industry as a whole to the number of workers employed by A.B.C., we can estimate the average number of separations per month in the plant at approximately 315 for the period from May, 1946 through June, 1947. Since the turnover rate in the plant during August and September, 1946 was about the same as that for the city as a whole, there is no reason to think it would have varied significantly from the rate for all industries at any other time during 1946 and 1947.

workers with some service might expect to be assigned to the better jobs
when they became available or were created, and new workers might look
forward to moving up through the hierarchy of desirability eventually.

There did appear in fact to be a rough pattern of movement from the
lower to the upper levels of the hierarchy which was facilitated by management policies and practices. This pattern did not follow a single upward
course from line assembly to machine operation to some other production
job to off-production work. Most new workers were assigned either to line
assembly or to machine operation, though a few were occasionally placed
directly in some off-production job. From the line or machine, men moved
either to a more desirable production job or to an off-production assignment. A few men moved from line assembly to machine operation and then
either to off-production or some other production classification. But there
appeared to be little mobility between the two top levels of the hierarchy
of desirability. Table 8 shows the patterns of advancement of the off-

Table 8

JOB MOBILITY IN THE A.B.C. PLANT OF OFF-PRODUCTION AND
MISCELLANEOUS PRODUCTION WORKERS

Pattern of mobility	Number
Line to off-production job	6
Line to miscellaneous production job	5
	11
Machine to off-production job	4
Machine to miscellaneous production job	2
	6
Line to machine to off-production job	3
Line to machine to miscellaneous production job	2
	5
Started on off-production job	5
Started on miscellaneous production job	1
	6
Total	28

production and miscellaneous production workers who were interviewed.
Nine of the twenty-eight workers included were wartime upgraders; their
wartime experience is not included in the table since it did not represent a
pattern of job mobility that would occur under normal circumstances.
Movement from one job to another on the same level of the hierarchy is
similarly omitted. Six workers started as machine-operators and moved on
to either off-production or miscellaneous production jobs; eleven began on
the line before securing more desirable jobs; five went from the line to a

machine before securing either off-production or other production work; and six began with desirable production or off-production jobs.

Movement from level to level in the hierarchy of desirability was governed by the formal seniority rule in those few instances in which the order of preference coincided with the nonskilled wage hierarchy. The line-tender knew that if he remained on the job long enough (five years, suggested one), his seniority might enable him to become a line repairman; the machine-operator might similarly become a machine-setter. But in most cases, movement in the hierarchy depended upon seniority in an informal sense and upon the worker's ability to utilize the transfer machinery created by the union contract.

Even when not bound by the formal seniority rule, management frequently respects length of service, though not necessarily in strict order of seniority, in filling desirable jobs. In reassigning workers after the war, for example, management gave those with substantial seniority their choice of jobs. This explains in part why ten of eighteen off-production workers and eight of ten miscellaneous production workers had prewar seniority, as compared with seven of the nineteen line assemblers and machine-operators. Even under ordinary circumstances, management gives workers already in the plant some priority over newly hired employees in filling desirable jobs made available by turnover or created by plant expansion. According to the union contract:

> It is the policy of Management to cooperate in every practical way with employees who desire transfers to new positions or vacancies in their department. Accordingly, such employees who make application to their foreman or the Personnel Department stating their desires, qualifications and experience, will be given preference for openings in their department provided they are capable of doing the job. However, employees who have made application as provided for above and who are capable of doing the job available shall be given preference for the openings in their department over new hires. Any secondary job openings resulting from filling jobs pursuant to this provision may be filled through promotion; or through transfer without regard to seniority standing, or by new hire.

In practice, workers may also apply to the Personnel Department for transfer from one department or division to another as well as within a department.

Length of service may indirectly facilitate workers' efforts to gain transfer under this contract provision. As they acquire experience over a period of years in different jobs,* their applications for transfer are likely to be given

---

* "Shifts in occupation are a normal part of the evolutionary process of the industry." Court, *Men, Methods and Machines in Automobile Manufacturing*, p. 13. Of the sixty-two workers interviewed, only some skilled workers and seven nonskilled workers who had been in the plant for only a short time had been confined to only one kind of work.

favorable consideration. Management is likely to look upon them as workers who will learn new jobs more quickly and be more proficient than other workers without comparable experience. Training time for most nonskilled jobs is sufficiently short so that to the outsider the range of variation in how long it takes to learn a new assignment and in the quality of performance is small. But to most workers and to management, even small differences in proficiency at routine tasks are readily apparent. (Line assemblers and machine-operators frequently referred to co-workers as "skilled," even though their jobs were of the usual routine sort. In this context, however, skilled meant the evident proficiency with which workers performed their tasks rather than the nature of the tasks themselves.) To management, these small differences obviously are important.

The existence of a formal transfer policy and of machinery through which workers can apply for desirable jobs places some of the responsibility for movement in the hierarchy in their own hands. Within the limits imposed by unpredictable changes in plant technology which sometimes eliminate desirable jobs,* workers had some room for the exercise of individual effort and the manipulation of the institutional machinery. "You do get a chance," said a truck-driver with seven years of service who had once worked on the line. "If you see a job you want, you make application for it and they do pretty good in giving men the jobs they want." Other workers, however, whose experience had not been as happy, were more skeptical of management's practices.

But for workers to take advantage of the policy of preference for men already in the plant, they had to know what the desirable jobs were, where they were, and when they became available. Applications for specific job openings were more likely to be successful than general requests for transfer to departments or divisions in which there might be no immediate vacancies. Since the hierarchy of desirability among nonskilled jobs had no official standing, there was no way in which information about job openings was regularly and systematically spread throughout the plant. Workers, therefore, had to rely upon informal channels of communication for job information.

The acquisition of knowledge about jobs and opportunities and of familiarity with informal communication lines was largely a function of time and, in a sense, therefore, of seniority. According to several old-timers,

---

* One worker who had been an upgrader-toolmaker during the war found himself on the paint line despite ten years of seniority because of such changes. After the war he had been reduced to a nonskilled maintenance job, one he had chosen because of its desirability. After a few months a change in the layout of his department had eliminated his job. By that time, all the other desirable jobs had been taken and he was arbitrarily assigned to the paint line. Even his seniority was of no help to him in these circumstances.

it took at least two or three years to "learn the ropes." Workers became familiar with the hierarchy of desirability in short order, if they did not know it beforehand. It took somewhat longer to learn which specific jobs in production divisions were particularly desirable. And it took even longer to establish relationships with strategically placed workers—the union committeemen, line repairmen, skilled maintenance workers—whose greater mobility in the plant made them the carriers of news and information. The time needed might be shortened if one had grown up close to the factory and had acquired plant know-how before going to work there, or if one had had previous experience in other automobile plants.

Workers who have avoided or escaped from the assembly line or the machine and who have achieved off-production or desirable production jobs have nothing further to which to look forward on the level of nonskilled labor except general wage increases or promotion to better-paying jobs of the same kind. The possibilities of the latter are uncertain and unpredictable, except in long-range terms, and they offer, in any case, only slight financial advancement. It is therefore hardly surprising that many workers with comparatively desirable jobs professed to have no job goals in the plant. Twelve of the eighteen men performing off-production assignments and five of the ten with desirable production jobs had no specific objectives in the factory. To these must be added five machine-operators and two line-tenders who, for various reasons, had no job goals in the plant, for a total of twenty-four of the forty-seven nonskilled workers interviewed.

These twenty-four nonskilled workers without factory job goals fall into three relatively distinct groups. Ten workers stressed the apparent lack of opportunity in the factory. They derived little satisfaction from their jobs but nevertheless had resigned themselves with varying degrees of frustration and resentment to the fact that they could expect nothing better in the factory.

Eight workers were satisfied with the jobs they held and with what they had managed to achieve in the plant. Their attitude was summed up in the comment of a forty-three-year-old fender-wrapper in parts and service who had been in the plant for fourteen years:

> My job's O.K. It's nice clean work and not too heavy and you work pretty regular. You don't make as much as in some other jobs but you work pretty steady so that by the time the year is over you come out all right. I've always had a pretty good job and I've never worked too hard and I've worked pretty steady.

A third group of six workers, which included the two line-tenders and two of the five machine-operators without job goals in the factory, paid little heed to plant alternatives chiefly because of their strong orientation toward out-of-the-shop goals. Three of these six workers, however, might not have been so intent on leaving if they felt that there were real opportunities for advancement in the factory.

No personal characteristics such as seniority, age, education, previous job experience, or parent's occupation distinguished those who were satisfied from those who were frustrated and resentful. The differences in their responses to the same objective circumstances—a comparatively good job and little likelihood of anything better—must be found in more subtle characteristics of personality, previous experience, and personal life context than were explored in this study. It is worth noting, however, that two workers in the satisfied group were machine-operators in their sixties who were engaged in the kind of work at which they had spent their occupational lives. They had no job goals because they were looking forward to the day when they could retire. Their satisfaction was based upon the knowledge that their seniority assured them of a job until they left the factory for the last time.

In comparison with both the satisfied and the frustrated, those workers who were intent on leaving the factory were younger, better educated, and had little seniority; four were in their twenties, one was thirty-eight and one forty-eight. Of the eighteen others without job goals in the factory, only two were in their twenties, four were in their thirties, and the others were over forty. Five of the six intent on leaving were high-school graduates; only five of the other eighteen had completed high school. One of the six held prewar seniority, one had come into the plant during the war, four after the war; eleven of the others were hired before the war, four were hired during the war, and only three had come into the plant after the war. In addition, the parents of five of these six workers were either white-collar employees or small businessmen. The two older workers (one of whom was the exception with regard to both education and prewar seniority) had held white-collar salaried jobs before coming into the factory. In both cases their parents were small businessmen.

These suggestive differences between workers who had no job goals in the factory because of out-of-the-shop aspirations and the others without factory objectives can only be understood after we have examined workers' attitudes toward leaving the factory and toward out-of-the-shop alternatives, a task to which we shall turn in Chapter VII. These six workers were by no means the only ones to talk of leaving. Indeed, forty-eight of the sixty-two workers interviewed (thirty-eight of the forty-seven nonskilled) answered affirmatively to the question: "Have you ever thought of getting out of the shop?" While six held no job goals in the factory chiefly because of their other interests, it is possible that other workers have out-of-the-shop goals because of their dissatisfaction with work in the factory, or that they simultaneously entertain various alternatives both in and out of the plant.

Footnotes to Chapter VI

1. Court: *Men, Methods and Machines in Automobile Manufacturing*, p. 13.
2. B. Leyson: *Automotive Occupations*, New York, E. P. Dutton & Co., Inc., 1941, pp. 69–71.
3. See, for example, F. J. Roethlisberger and W. J. Dickson: *Management and the Worker*, Cambridge, Harvard University Press, 1940, and L. G. Reynolds and J. Shister: *Job Horizons*, New York, Harper & Brothers, 1949.
4. See Reynolds and Shister, *op. cit.*, p. 11, and T. V. Purcell: *The Worker Speaks His Mind*, Cambridge, Harvard University Press, 1953, pp. 124–134.
5. The importance of social relationships on the job in determining morale has been richly documented in recent years. The classic study in this area is Roethlisberger and Dickson, *op. cit.* See also E. Mayo: *Human Problems of an Industrial Civilization*, New York, The Macmillan Company, 1933, and *Social Problems of an Industrial Civilization*, Cambridge, Graduate School of Business Administration, Harvard University, 1945.

VII

Out of the Factory

Interest in the possibility of leaving the factory ran high among the workers interviewed and out-of-the-shop goals were frequently discussed in the day-to-day talk of men in the plant. We have already noted that forty-eight of the sixty-two workers interviewed answered in the affirmative to the question: "Have you ever thought of getting out of the shop?" A dozen workers spontaneously remarked that "everybody" or "a majority of the fellows" or some substantial proportion such as eighty or ninety per cent wished to leave the factory. Even among the fourteen who reported that they had not thought of leaving, one occasionally heard the wistful remark: "Not now, but someday, if I can, I'd like to."

Most of the talk of leaving dealt with the traditional avenue of success, some kind of small business venture. Of the forty-eight who had thought of quitting, thirty-one suggested a "business of my own" as their goal. Six workers wished to become independent farmers.* Three wanted to secure selling or office jobs outside the factory, one had applied for admission to the local police force, two younger workers said that they intended to go to college in order to prepare for semiprofessional careers, one was taking a correspondence course in cartooning before trying to sell his work, one spoke of embarking upon evangelical work for his church (a largely working-class Protestant denomination), and three merely wanted other kinds of wage jobs.

This widespread interest in leaving the factory stemmed chiefly from dissatisfaction with work in the plant rather than from strong commitments to out-of-the-shop goals. These men saw in business or farming an escape from the disabilities of factory work, not an opportunity to become wealthy.

The generalized attributes of life in a large mass-production plant con-

---

* It is probable that greater interest in farming exists among workers in the plant than is suggested by this small number. For reasons given in Chapter III, the workers interviewed did not include a proportionate number of rural and small-town residents (who numbered about one-third of the plant work force) from whom might have come a larger number of men oriented toward the possibility of farming.

stantly stimulated the desire to leave the factory among workers in all job categories. Workers with less desirable jobs, those on the assembly line, for example, were, it is true, somewhat more likely to want to leave than others, and, as we noted earlier, the turnover rate was highest among assembly-line workers. Only four of twenty-nine production workers had not thought of leaving, compared with five of eighteen off-production workers and five of fifteen skilled tradesmen. But as these figures indicate, a substantial majority in each job classification, including the skilled employees who earned the highest wages and did the most respected and rewarding work, spoke of their desire to "get out of the shop."

Workers might feel, as did one of those interviewed, that they have "the best job in the shop," while they simultaneously complained: "There's no future in the factory," and "There's no interest in a job in the factory." Workers limited their demands in the plant to adequate wages, some measure of security, and the avoidance of physical and psychological strain and discomfort. But even when these demands were met workers frequently complained that they could see no "future" in the factory and they displayed feelings about their work which can best be summed up in the concept of *alienation*.

The complaint that there is no future in the factory carried two distinct meanings, that there is no opportunity for advancement of a traditional sort, and that workers cannot count on a secure position in the plant as age gradually drains them of strength and energy.* The objective basis for the first meaning emerges clearly from the analysis in Chapter IV. Their likely fate in the plant as they grow older is less clearly visible.

Uncertainties concerning the future stem only in small part from the possibility of layoff because of age, although the industry was once notorious for its practice of discharging older workers who could no longer maintain the pace set by the machine and the line.[1] This practice has been largely checked by several provisions of the union contract: layoffs must follow seniority, with those most recently hired being the first laid off; rehiring after a layoff must begin with those with the longest seniority and proceed according to length of service; if workers feel that they are unjustly laid off or are not called back in accordance with the provisions of the contract, they may file a grievance which can be carried all the way to an impartial arbitrator. Despite these safeguards, some of the workers interviewed felt that management might try to get rid of older workers by refusing to take

---

* In his recent study of automobile workers' aspirations, R. Guest also found that "lack of advancement opportunity" and "fear of not being able to keep up the pace of work because of age" contributed to workers' desire to leave the plant. "Work Careers and Aspirations of Automobile Workers," *Amer. Sociol. Review* 19:155–163 (April, 1954).

them back after a layoff, on the grounds that they could no longer do the work required of them. A few such cases in the spring of 1946, whatever their merits, had stimulated this fear.

Even if they are not laid off, however, older workers face an uncertain future in the plant. As they lose their capacity for sustained strenuous effort, they may have to take other jobs in the factory which pay less and are held in some measure of disrepute, for most jobs do require considerable physical exertion. The only alternative may be dismissal because they actually cannot do the work. The living examples of this job fate frequently generate a desire for some other alternative outside the plant. A forty-year-old line repairman commented, for example:

> You see the fellows who have been there for years who are now sweeping. That's why most of the fellows want to get out. Like you take Jim, he's been there for thirty years and now he's sweeping. When you aren't any good any more, they discard you like an old glove.

An inspector in his late thirties declared:

> I'm going to quit the shop. I've been there for twelve years and what have I got from it. And if I stay there for another twelve years, what have I got to look forward to? When I get to be fifty they'll make a sweeper out of me. That's nothing to look forward to. I might as well take a chance on something else.

(Shortly thereafter this worker did leave in order to become a salesman for a national company which distributed novelties to drug, candy, and grocery stores.)

Beyond the prospect of relegation to poorly paid jobs with low status is the problem of what to do when one becomes old enough to want or need to retire. These workers could not expect to save enough from their earnings in most cases to provide for their old age; federal social-security payments insure only a bare minimum. Five workers had therefore focussed their interest upon some kind of business which might provide at least a minimum income without requiring effort beyond their capacity. It is interesting to note that the only two workers who took seriously the maxim to "build a better mousetrap" were men in their sixties who were worried about how they would support themselves when they finally left the plant. They were tinkering with small gadgets which they hoped to market. But they lacked the necessary capital and were looking for someone who would be willing and able to provide financial backing.

The establishment of a company pension plan in 1950 undoubtedly lifted this fear from the minds of many workers. Indeed, it is quite possible that the existence of a company pension will tie workers closely to their present employment. But the lack of opportunity for individual advancement, as well as other disabilities, remains.

Even if they gain some measure of security, both present and future, nonskilled workers in a large, highly mechanized plant such as A.B.C., can secure little significant experience of themselves as productive human beings. They are *alienated*, we may say, from themselves and their work. Labor in such a plant has become, in Marx's words, "not the satisfaction of a need but only the means to satisfy the needs outside it." The tools and machines which workers use or operate, the visible symbols of the craftsman's identity, belong to others. Workers have no claim to the goods they produce; in that respect they are alienated from the fruits of their labor. Although automobile workers, unlike many other industrial workers, can recognize the finished product to which they have contributed, their contribution is so small because of the extensive division of labor, and so insignificant because of the substitution of machines for manual skill, that the psychological tie between worker and product is tenuous enough to be almost meaningless.

Going to work in a large mechanized plant entails the surrender of control over their own actions for those hours for which workers are paid; that they can be paid by the hour is itself evidence of external domination and separation from the product. In most jobs machines set the tempo and rhythm of work. In all jobs workers must submit to the authority of those in whom control is vested by the organization, with only the indirect influence of the union as a check upon the power of management.

To a lesser degree this process of alienation affects the skilled workers as well. They too do not own most of the tools they use; they have no claim on the goods they must produce; they are subject to the authority of management. And in a large plant they too are subject to the anonymity and impersonality of a complex bureaucratic organization.

These features of work in mass-production industry which alienate the worker from his labor and from himself lead to deprivations which are not easily verbalized. Yet they do show themselves in various ways: in the sad comment, "The only reason a man works is to make a living"; in the occasional overflow of resentment, "Sometimes you feel like jamming things up in the machine and saying good-bye to it"; in the cynical observation, "The things I like best about my job are quitting time, pay day, days off, and vacations"; in the complaint, "There's no interest in a job in the shop"; and in the resigned answer to questions about their work, "A job's a job."

These suggestions of deep-seated frustrations or deprivations require more intensive research than has been possible in this study. Yet it seems probable that the alienation of these workers does much to explain their widespread interest in small business and, to a lesser extent, farming, and their responsiveness to the values of the small-business tradition. Paradoxically, the very process of alienation which Marx thought would transform industrial workers into class-conscious proletarians has instead stimulated their interest in small business and in small-scale private farming, institutions of capitalist society which Marx asserted were doomed to extinction. Indeed, Lipset and Bendix have recently suggested that of all groups in America, industrial workers respond most vigorously to the small-business tradition.[2] Empirical support for this hypothesis comes from the finding of a 1940 *Fortune* poll that "The desire to run a business is highest in the low income brackets where the immediate prospects for its fulfillment are probably least."[3]

In both small business and farming workers see an opportunity to gain what they rarely achieve in the factory, a rich and full sense of self. The variety of tasks and the individual control of the tempo at which one works in a business or on a farm contrast favorably in the workers' eyes with routine factory jobs. The traditional stress upon "independence" and the desirability of "being one's own boss" strikes a resonant chord among workers subject to the authority of the organization and the mechanical domination of the machine. A machine operator who had been in the plant for four years testified:

> The main thing is to be independent and give your own orders and not have to take them from anybody else. That's the reason the fellows in the shop all want to start their own business. Then the profits are all for yourself. When you're in the shop there's nothing in it for yourself. When you put in a screw or a head on a motor, there's nothing for yourself in it. So you just do what you have to in order to get along. A fellow would rather do it for himself. If you expend the energy, it's for your own benefit then.

"There is a satisfaction in working for yourself," said one skilled worker, "knowing that you're building something up."

For some workers, however, the attraction of farming in part lies in its character as a way of life with intrinsic gratifications as well as in its role as a way of making a living. "I like to see things grow," said one line-tender in explaining his interest in farming. "I think it's better for the kids to grow up on a farm than in the city," said another with four small children. "It's just my way of living," said a third. Four workers wanted to farm despite unsuccessful efforts to do so in the past. Two others, with no direct farming experience, had idealized farm life as a satisfying alternative to that of the urban industrial worker.

Because talk of leaving the factory may not betoken deeply held ambitions, resolute intentions, and concrete plans, but may be "just talk," one must dig beneath the expressions of interest and desire with which we have thus far been concerned to the levels of intention and action. When workers were asked if they had made any concrete plans or taken any definite steps toward achievement of out-of-the-shop goals, for example, conscientious saving, exploring alternative business possibilities, looking for a farm to buy or for a more desirable job elsewhere, many quickly qualified their desire with reasons why they could not leave the factory. We can then separate those workers who were actively concerned with out-of-the-shop goals from those who were just talking. Of the thirty-one interested in the possibility of a business of some kind, twenty-two did not expect to leave the factory, nor did three of the six prospective farmers and eight of the remaining thirteen. Of the seventeen who insisted that they intended to leave, only eight had gone past the stage of wishful thinking and escapist dreams: the two older workers who had been tinkering with gadgets, the one young man who had applied for the local police force, the two young men who had applied for admission to college, a toolmaker who had been slowly buying machinery for a small tool-and-die shop set up in his garage, a nonskilled worker who was conscientiously saving as much as he could to buy a farm, and another nonskilled worker who was actively looking for some kind of small business venture.

The seventeen who insisted that they intended to get out of the factory tended to have less seniority and to be younger than those who felt they could not manage to leave the plant. Eight of the seventeen had been hired after the war, compared with only two of the thirty-one who were just talking. Six of the seventeen were in their twenties, four in their thirties; only four of the thirty-one were in their twenties, while fifteen were in their thirties. Of the eight workers with concrete plans, four were in their twenties, one was thirty, and one thirty-one, and two were in their sixties. Five of the eight had been in the factory for less than a year.

In June, 1951, eleven of the seventeen who had intended to leave were still in the factory. Three of those with definite plans when interviewed had achieved their goals. These three workers possessed little seniority (less than a year in each case) and were all in their twenties when interviewed. One had registered in the local college, one had become a policeman, and one had successfully opened his own tool-and-die shop. One who had intended to go into business had taken another job elsewhere; one who had wanted a better job had left, only to return to the factory two years later, and one sixty-two-year-old worker was no longer in the plant, although no information was available as to his whereabouts.

These data suggest the hypothesis that many men who come to work in the plant while still in their twenties or, perhaps, early thirties, define their jobs as temporary and do not expect to remain. Some do leave, but the longer the others remain in the plant, the less likely are they to muster the initiative to leave, despite the continual talk of doing so. We shall examine this hypothesis in greater detail in Chapter IX, when we attempt to suggest the more or less typical chronology of aspirations of automobile workers during the course of their occupational career.

The gap between desire and action evident among many workers was rooted in the concrete problems faced by men whose aspirations were focussed on small business and farming. Because both business and farming have become highly mechanized and capitalized, it is hardly possible for the "prudent, penniless beginner in the world," to "labor for wages awhile, save a surplus with which to buy tools or land for himself, then labor on his own account for awhile and at length hire another new beginner to help him." Opportunities for workers to go into business do exist; in a recent study in California, over twenty per cent of all manual workers interviewed had at one time been in a business of their own.[4] Seven of those interviewed in Autotown had once owned their own business (seven others had once owned or rented farms), and the local labor weekly frequently reported about workers who had gone into business for themselves, usually with recommendations that they be patronized. But the opportunities in business for men with little capital are primarily in the fields of distribution and service in which competition is severe and the business mortality rate high. For the individual entrepreneur, for the automobile worker, for example, with only his personal savings, or those of relatives, to invest in machinery, fixtures, or the purchase of a small farm, the risks are almost inordinately high.

We have no detailed data on business opportunities in Autotown or the surrounding area, but it is possible, by using data for the entire state and the limited information available about the city and the county in which it is located, to make some rough estimates for the period during which this study was carried on. Table 9 gives the number of businesses in the state in each of the major industry divisions, as of March 31 of each year from 1944 through 1948. It also indicates the number of new and discontinued businesses each year during that period. Retail-trade and service industries obviously dominate the business population with over two-thirds of the total. The number of businesses increased by approximately 32,000 from 1944 to 1948 with almost 18,000 of that total in retail and service establishments. Almost 87,000 new businesses opened but over 55,000 closed their

Table 9

NUMBER OF BUSINESSES IN THE STATE BY MAJOR INDUSTRY DIVISIONS, MARCH 31,
1944–1948; NEW AND DISCONTINUED BUSINESSES, 1944–1948.

(*In thousands*)

Major Industry Division	1944	1945	1946	1947	1948
Contract construction	7.7	7.6	10.6	12.5	13.9
Manufacturing	10.4	10.6	11.8	13.4	13.1
Wholesale trade	5.3	5.5	6.2	6.7	6.9
Retail trade	63.8	64.0	69.1	74.2	74.5
Service industries	26.0	26.7	29.4	32.4	33.1
All other	13.1	13.5	15.0	16.2	16.9
Totals	126.3	128.0	142.1	155.4	158.5
New Businesses	10.4	16.0	26.7	16.9	16.9
Discontinued Businesses	9.5	8.3	9.4	11.5	16.2

Source: "State Estimates of the Business Population," *Survey of Current Business*, December, 1949, pp. 8–17.

doors. While not all business fatalities were new firms, it seems probable that most of those which did close were postwar ventures that were started with little capital.

From these figures and the available data about Autotown and its county it seems likely that from 1944 through 1948 approximately 1,700 new businesses were opened in the county (which had a total population of approximately 170,000) and about 1,100 were discontinued. Approximately 1,100 were started in the city and about seven hundred closed. During that period, there was a net increase of about twenty in the number of manufacturing enterprises in the county; in 1947, according to the Census of Manufactures, there were 181 such firms. The number of service establishments probably increased by about one hundred and the number of retail stores in the county by approximately two hundred. The 1948 Census of Business reported 441 service establishments and 1,582 retail stores in the county. Most of the manufacturing enterprises, about seventy per cent of the service establishments, and sixty per cent of the retail stores were located in the city.

Although many men did manage to start businesses in the first postwar years, particularly during 1946, the odds against a lasting success, as our data indicate, were very high. By 1948 almost as many businesses were failing as were opening.

In farming, opportunities were even more limited than in business. The total number of farms in Autotown's county and in the surrounding six counties—those into which A.B.C. workers might venture—has steadily decreased. Between 1940 and 1945, the number of farms in these counties fell from 21,725 to 20,149. During those years the total acreage included in farms increased slightly, so that the average farm increased from 107 to 111 acres. Concomitantly, farm values in these seven counties rose by about fifty per cent to approximately seventy-five dollars per acre, thus increasing substantially the necessary initial investment. One worker who hoped to buy a farm estimated that it might take him ten years, if he were reasonably fortunate, to save enough money to buy a profitable one.

Comparatively few automobile workers possessed the savings necessary to initiate a business which might have a good chance to survive successfully or to buy a reasonably profitable farm, even in 1945 when savings were at a peak because of the preceding four years of steady work and frequent overtime.* By and large, workers had to "start on a shoestring," as more than one of those who were interviewed put it, with the attendant high risks. Detailed data on the savings of the workers who were interviewed or of automobile workers in general are not available. But one gained the impression, supported by officers of the credit union to which workers in the plant belonged, that comparatively few men possessed more than a few hundred dollars in cash or government bonds, and few other assets except for their homes and their automobiles. One worker boasted, for example, that he "had a lot of money in the bank, about eleven hundred dollars." Other data available in studies of liquid-asset holdings, that is, government securities and bank accounts, of various income and occupational groups in the United States, suggest the limited sums available to most automobile workers for investment in a business or farm. Average weekly earnings of automobile workers in 1945 were $51.99, a figure which indicates that a large proportion of them earned from two to three thousand dollars that year. The median value of liquid-asset holdings among those in this income group early in 1946 was only $470. Only a quarter of those in this group had liquid assets of more than $1,090.[5] Early in 1947, after a year of lower earnings (automobile workers averaged only $50.61 per week in 1946), the median value of liquid-asset holdings of skilled and semiskilled workers was only $400.[6]

These limited resources are reflected in the concrete business goals in which the workers interviewed expressed interest, and in the kinds of farms would-be farmers talked of buying. In addition to six workers who talked of some kind of small store, otherwise undefined, two men wished to open or buy grocery stores, one a feed store, one a woman's clothing shop, one a bakery, one a small restaurant. Three others hoped to open automobile-

---

* Many workers had invested their wartime savings in the purchase of a home or in paying off the mortgage on a home. As we shall see later (p. 126), not only have these workers focussed some of their most deeply held sentiments on home ownership, they have also given home ownership an important role in their definition of advancement and getting ahead.

repair shops. Six workers expressed interest in what is probably a local or regional idiosyncrasy: they wanted to buy some "tourist property" in the relatively undeveloped area of the state "up north." They would then earn their living by selling supplies to the hunters and fishermen who came to the area, by renting cabins which they proposed to build themselves, and, if they could find desirable lake-front property, by renting boats to fishermen. This more or less utopian goal combined the desire for independence with the recreational interests of many workers. One assembly-line worker felt that he knew enough about carpentry because he had once built a house for himself to try his hand as an independent artisan. Finally, as we have noted earlier, two workers had developed gadgets which they hoped to market, and six skilled workers talked of opening their own tool-and-die shops. Of all these alternatives, the last required the greatest capital. Although skilled workers were obviously more likely to be able to save because of their higher wages and more regular employment, there is some question as to whether even they could save enough to buy the relatively expensive equipment needed in a modern machine shop.

So expensive were profitable farms in the Autotown area that all but one of the prospective farmers interviewed talked of buying small marginal farms which might be operated in a limited fashion while they were still working in the factory. The extent to which this pattern of part-time farming and full-time work does occur is suggested in the following data for Autotown's county for 1945: Of 2,228 farms, 702 were less than thirty acres, 714 produced goods worth less than eight hundred dollars during the year; 759 of 2,951 farm-operators worked more than 250 days off the farm during the year. One prospective farmer detailed his plans as follows:

> I figure I'll start just like I bought this house of mine [which he had bought eight years earlier for $1,600, of which he had only paid eight hundred dollars up to 1948]—on a shoestring. I'll mortgage this place, then make a down payment on the farm. When I first go on the farm, though, I won't quit the shop. I'll rent out the fields and that'll pay for the farm while my wages will support my family. I figure in two years I ought to have five head of cattle and a tractor. I'll have to work hard, get some more savings, sacrifice some.

But when interviewed this worker had practically no savings, and he complained that he was unable to put aside any money each week after paying the normal family bills. The difficulties inherent in this plan were clearly recognized and critically looked upon by many others, as evidenced in the following verses from a poem which appeared in the local labor weekly:

> The odor of the barn yard
> Where milk turned into beef
> Comes wafting back to me again
> Right here at [A.B.C.].

> Our country minded workers
> Who try to raise their meat
> Now come to work with eyes half closed
> Too tired to scrape their feet.
>
> And after working here all day,
> They till the soil with care.
> They think they'll find a pot of gold
> Awaiting them out there.
>
> They talk about retiring,
> To me it's just a yarn.
> We'll have them with us many years,
> Still talking about their farm.

One worker intended to wait until he was able to buy a farm on which he could count for a reasonable income, no matter how long it would take, rather than try to work in the factory and farm at the same time. He had tried to operate a farm while working in the plant during the war, but had found it so difficult that he sold out and moved back to the city.

Because of a deep concern with security many workers were reluctant to face the uncertainties of marginal farming and of the kinds of small businesses to which most men necessarily confined their interest. Twenty-one workers, all of whom had been in the plant more than five years and thirteen of whom had been in the plant more than ten years, said explicitly that they would be unwilling to sacrifice the security they enjoyed for the doubtful prospects of business or farming. They all knew of others who had given up their seniority in order to start a business, buy a farm, or even to take a seemingly better job, only to return to the factory when the business failed, the farm yielded only a meager livelihood, or the job provided no improvement. Those who thus returned no longer had the assurance that they would not be laid off immediately when production was cut down; they now had to wait longer to be called back after a layoff; they had no claim to promotion to better-paying jobs or to otherwise more desirable assignments in the plant. As a forty-year-old line repairman with twelve years of seniority explained:

> I can't afford to leave now. I can be pretty sure of working if the plant is working. There'll be layoffs, but 1935 seniority is coming to be pretty good now. And if you're willing to do whatever work there is, they can always find something for you.

And all twenty-one men were old enough to have experienced directly the impact of the Great Depression, whose persistent overtones colored their feelings about holding on to a steady job. "I can remember," said a thirty-two-year-old stock-picker who had never worked anywhere else, "when you couldn't buy a job. These young fellows nowadays don't appreciate seniority."

Undoubtedly strong feelings about risk and uncertainty stem in some cases from doubts as to one's abilities in business or farming, or from pressure from wives and families. (Conversely, one might expect that those who seriously intended to leave the factory or who actually did so were encouraged or stimulated to ambitious efforts by their wives or families.) It seems a plausible hypothesis that many workers, with no more than a high-school education at best, and with little or no experience except factory work, will not be confident of their abilities in a field as uncertain as small business;* and that the women whom industrial workers marry will be more likely to insist on maintaining some degree of security than to encourage enterprise and risk.

In some cases workers felt that their family responsibilities weighed too heavily for them to risk the loss of the security they enjoyed or whatever savings they possessed. "You can't think of getting out of the shop," said a forty-two-year-old machine-operator with four children, the oldest fifteen, the youngest seven. "You've got family responsibilities and they come first." In a few cases, the accident of personal tragedy with its unexpected demands added particular weight to these responsibilities. For example, a truck-driver who wished to be a farmer could only talk wistfully of his hopes; his only son had been born deaf and he felt he had to remain in Autotown where there was a special school for handicapped children. A would-be businessman had seen his savings disappear when his wife was forced to spend two years in a tuberculosis sanitarium.

The desire to hold on to the security they had gained through seniority also explains in part the relative lack of interest in better jobs elsewhere and the unwillingness of all but one of those who wanted a different job to quit. Said an inspector with six years of seniority who had gone to college and would have preferred white-collar employment:

> Suppose I get a better job. I work for a year and then something happens, the job folds up or something, and I'm out of work. As long as I stay here I can be pretty sure of working. I've got a family and I can't take chances.

To this concern with security must be added the fact that the A.B.C. plant pays comparatively high wages. We have already seen that wages in the automobile industry have been higher than in most industries. And A.B.C. reputedly paid higher wages than any of the other large plants in Autotown. "Where else can I work and make as much money?" queried

---

* We suggested earlier that a lack of self-confidence might play an important role in workers' feelings about advancement in the factory. See p. 59.

a machine-operator who had not completed high school and had never worked elsewhere. The one worker who seriously wished to shift jobs was disgruntled and bitter because he had been assigned to the assembly line despite twelve years of seniority and experience on many other jobs.

Some workers, whatever the pressures upon them to leave the factory, avoid the problems inherent in moving from one kind of work or one job to another. They are unwilling to give up the security of familiar routines and established relations with their co-workers, for they would then face problems in adjusting to different circumstances, learning fresh routines, and establishing new relationships with others. The present job may have all the inadequacies of an old shoe, it may offer weak support, have little style and no future, but it may, at least, be comfortable.

In June, 1951, seventeen of these twenty-one workers who felt that they could not risk loss of their seniority were still in the factory as wage workers. One skilled worker in the group had been promoted to foremanship, another skilled worker had taken a similar job in a plant in another city, and no data were available for two workers no longer in the plant (both of whom had been over fifty years old when interviewed).

It seems clear from our preceding analysis that talk of leaving the factory and interest in out-of-the-shop goals are related in relatively few instances to positive action. Their major significance undoubtedly lies in the social and psychological functions they serve for workers in a large mechanized plant. Undoubtedly talk of leaving the factory is in large part merely a form of the normal griping which one might expect not only from non-skilled factory labor but also from businessmen and professionals, from clerks, salesmen, and skilled workers. As such, its chief function is as a safety valve for tensions generated by the day's work. Its prevalence and persistence among automobile workers testify to the constant irritations found in their jobs. Sometimes tensions do explode in an abrupt quitting. But as pressures to hold their jobs increase with age and growing family responsibility, the quick impulse is more likely to be restrained. Pent-up feelings are released in talk.

Out-of-the-shop goals provide the stuff of utopian daydreams which make present difficulties more tolerable. "It makes the time go quicker and easier when I keep thinking about that turkey farm I'd like to buy," said a fifty-year-old line-tender who also felt that he had to hang on to his present job because at his age finding another job would be difficult. A few minutes later he admitted that he could never hope to save enough money to buy his dreamed-of turkey farm. When interviewed a month later, he was day-dreaming about "tourist property up north." Even though hopes crumble when put to the test of reality, the talk and the daydreams they generate may soften the irritations and aggravations of the moment.

By emphasizing to their fellows the strength of their intentions and the ripeness of their plans, workers seek to elicit one another's respect. Since high value is placed upon achievement of out-of-the-shop goals, those who seem on the verge of leaving in order to start a business may gain increased prestige. Men spoke frequently and enviously of their co-workers who seemed near achievement of some out-of-the-shop goal. Yet concomitantly the spuriousness and unreality of much of this talk was frequently recognized, as is evident from the verses about worker-farmers quoted earlier. Talk of leaving may therefore be double-edged: on the one hand it may elicit respect, on the other it may stamp one as an idle and unrealistic fellow who talks too much.

Of particular importance from our point of view is the fact that talk of leaving the factory, particularly when focussed upon traditionally sanctioned goals, serves to reinforce the worker's identification with the dominant success values of American culture. Even if he recognizes, in those occasional moments when he looks at things clearly, the emptiness of his talk of buying tourist property or a turkey farm, the risks of failure in business, the likelihood of low income in an automobile-repair shop or a small grocery store, the automobile worker has not surrendered to the difficulties of his position. In his own mind he may appear to be persevering and hopeful, ambitious and hard working, just as he is encouraged to be. He too wants to get ahead as others have done before him and, perhaps, as his children will do after him. By seeking to convince others of the reality and strength of his aspirations, he fosters his belief in his own ambition and perseverance—and he continues to believe in the reality of opportunity. We shall return to this last function of talk of leaving the factory and of interest in out-of-the-shop goals in Chapter X when we examine what getting ahead and success actually mean to these automobile workers.

Footnotes to Chapter VII

1. See H. Harris: *American Labor*, New Haven, Yale University Press, 1939, p. 273; "Automobile Worker," *Fortune*, December, 1935, at p. 115; W. Haber and P. L. Stanchfield: *The Problem of Economic Insecurity in Michigan*, A Report to the State Emergency Relief Commission, Lansing, 1936, p. 68.
2. S. Lipset and R. Bendix: "Social Mobility and Occupational Career Patterns II. Social Mobility," *Amer. J. Sociol.* 57:494-504 (March, 1952).
3. *Fortune*, February, 1940, p. 28.
4. Lipset and Bendix, *op. cit.*, p. 503.
5. "A National Survey of Liquid Asset Distribution According to Income," *Federal Reserve Bulletin* 32:716-722 (July, 1946).
6. "Survey of Consumer Finances, Part II: Consumer Incomes and Liquid Asset Holdings," *Federal Reserve Bulletin* 33:788-802 (July, 1946).

VIII

Advancement via the Union

According to the newer version of the tradition of opportunity, the path to success lies within one or another of the great modern bureaucracies. In a society dominated by giant corporations, big government, and mass organizations, ascent within a bureaucratic hierarchy substitutes for the now dubious but not yet rejected small-business model of success. In the bureaucratic model, the ambitious, capable young man secures a thorough training, cultivates a pleasant personality, gains a position in a large firm, in government, or in some other organization, and then by dint of hard work and careful calculation makes his way to the top of the hierarchy.

We have already seen, however, that automobile workers without education and training possess few opportunities for advancement within the giant corporation for which they work, no matter how ambitious, capable, personable, or hard working they may be. With few exceptions they will remain on the level of wage labor as long as they are employed by this corporation—or any other large corporation. As we have already noted, this inability to secure advancement within the corporate hierarchy contributes to the still-lively interest in the older small-business tradition.

The governmental hierarchy offers no greater promise to automobile workers than does corporate enterprise. Because of their limited education, they can usually secure only various kinds of manual jobs in government which are likely to pay lower wages than work in the automobile industry. If they can pass the necessary examinations, they may be able to gain salaried positions as mailmen, post-office clerks, policemen, or firemen. For higher positions in government, as in industry, they must acquire advanced training, a possibility out of reach of all but a few young men without family responsibilities. Only one of the workers interviewed was directly interested in a government job, a twenty-four-year-old machine-operator who wished to become a policeman.

This one worker was a veteran, a high-school graduate, married, with an infant son. His father had been a nonskilled worker in the A.B.C. plant for many years, but had left after the war to become an insurance salesman. His wife had been employed as a clerk-secretary before their marriage and, until their child arrived, after their marriage. By his own lights, he was not "particularly ambitious." He saw in a policeman's job steady employment with life-long security at a reasonably good salary rather than an opportunity to become "successful" in a traditional sense.

Another machine-operator, a twenty-year-old unmarried worker, whose father was a used-car dealer and who was in the plant temporarily, intended to go to college to study police administration in preparation for a professional law-enforcement career. On the other hand, four workers who were interviewed had left government service in order to take factory jobs: two ex-mailmen, one ex-post-office clerk, and a former member of a road-repair crew. During the depression decade, the relative security of government employment made it appear particularly attractive; that attractiveness had waned during the war years of steady employment in private industry.

The one large organization which may hold out some promise of individual economic and social advancement without regard to previous education and training is the union. In building up the organizational apparatus necessary to achieve its goals and maintain its corporate existence, the United Automobile Workers, as well as other unions, has created a new avenue of mobility open primarily, although not exclusively, to factory workers.* Paradoxically, the collective pursuit of common goals has provided many individuals with opportunities for personal advancement. Within the union's formal structure, workers may climb to positions which offer more money, greater prestige, more interesting work, and more social power than they could gain from their jobs in the factory.† They can exchange the overalls and denim shirt for the business suit, white collar, and tie, the worker's schedule which may bring him to his job at 6:30 or 7:00 A.M. for a daily office schedule, and the need to punch a time clock for the freedom of individual responsibility. Today's labor leaders, C. Wright Mills has suggested, are America's most recent version of the self-made man.[1]

---

* The union's need for technically trained personnel—lawyers, economists, publicists—has also opened some positions within its ranks to persons, frequently of middle-class origin, who do not come from the factory ranks. Among professionals in some fields, the existence of career opportunities in unions is now widely recognized. Even a fashion magazine for college girls, for example, may on occasion offer its readers "Leads on Labor Jobs." See *Mademoiselle*, February, 1950, pp. 116-117.

† "Another important contribution of the labor movement is the provision of a new ladder by which the average boy or girl can rise to a position of influence. . . . Some twenty thousand men and women have risen to full time positions in leading their fellow workers." G. Watson, "Labor Unions and Morale," in G. Watson, Ed., *Civilian Morale*, New York, Society for the Psychological Study of Social Issues, 1942, p. 339.

The conventional view of trade-union leadership sees it as a "selfless calling" dedicated to the welfare of others, a view illustrated in a recent (July 16, 1952) editorial comment of *The New York Times*: "Trade union leadership is a 'cause' that has enlisted the untiring efforts of many unselfish men who have wished above all to help the worker improve his material and social well-being. It is not, and should not be, regarded as a business." The union's contemporary function as an avenue of mobility for individuals has been viewed critically because of a presumed conflict between the personal goals of union leaders and the collective goals of the organization. Labor racketeering is the most obvious form of union officials' self-aggrandizement at the expense of the membership, but some observers have suggested that even honest and devoted union leaders may change the policies they pursue as their greater income and different personal style of life give them middle-class status.[2]

We are concerned here, however, not with the consequences for union policies of the opportunities for individual advancement which are available in the union hierarchy, but with the nature of these opportunities, the pattern and prerequisites of advancement in the U.A.W., and the prevalent attitudes toward union leadership as a career. The data for this chapter are drawn not only from formal interviews with A.B.C. workers, but also from interviews with officers of the A.B.C. local and of other locals in Autotown and elsewhere, and from observation of the five U.A.W. locals in the city.

In Autotown, where the U.A.W. had approximately twelve thousand members in 1947, five men were on the payroll of one or another of the local unions. In the A.B.C. local, the largest in the city with about five thousand members, the president and the financial secretary were on the union payroll, devoting themselves completely to union affairs. Their salaries were somewhat greater than the earnings of most workers in the plant; in 1947, when weekly wages averaged about sixty dollars, the president's salary was seventy-five dollars per week, the financial secretary's slightly less. One former A.B.C. worker drew a full-time salary from the Autotown C.I.O. Council as editor of the local C.I.O. weekly newspaper.

Four men, one of whom also came from the A.B.C. local, constituted the staff of the international union in the city, drawing their salaries from the international treasury. They serviced the locals in Autotown as well as carrying on organization of any plants into which the union had not yet penetrated. Two other Autotown workers, both members of the A.B.C. local, were on the staff of the international union, one in Detroit in one of the central departments of the union, the other as a roving trouble-shooter for another department. International representatives, as all these salaried staff members were called, were appointed rather than elected. Their salaries in 1946 ranged from sixty to ninety dollars per week. (Salaries of international representatives were raised to seventy to one hundred dollars per week by the 1947 convention of the union.)

It is difficult to estimate accurately the total number of men and women who draw salaries from the U.A.W. (exclusive of secretarial staff who are not members of the union). In 1947, the international staff numbered about three hundred. A somewhat larger number were full-time salaried officers or staff members of local unions, drawing their salaries from local treasuries. Some locals were not large enough to support any salaried officers or staff, while others, such as the gigantic Ford Local 600 and Amalgamated Local 12 of Toledo, utilized the full-time services not only of several elective officers, but also of appointive officials who might be assigned to further organization, educational work, publications, or other union activities. Since each of the more than one thousand locals in the U.A.W. decides how many full-time salaried officials it wants to support, the total for all locals is not readily available.

If there were proportionately as many salaried officials in the union as a whole as there were in Autotown in 1947, the total, for a membership of approximately one million, would have come to about 835. In all probability, the total was somewhat larger, since the heaviest concentration of salaried staff was in Detroit where the largest locals were to be found and where the international offices, with their various service departments, were located.

By 1951 the union hierarchy had grown larger at what was probably an even greater rate than the union itself. The steady expansion of union functions requires an ever-larger staff; in 1951 there were slightly more than four hundred persons on the payroll of the international union, an increase of about one-third over 1947, while the membership had grown by about twenty-five per cent to approximately 1,250,000 dues-paying members. Concomitantly, the union's policy of encouraging the amalgamation of small locals unable to support salaried officers into larger locals which could "have a Union Hall, a full-time Financial Secretary and have a Business Agent and a place to meet and be able to do their work"[3] has probably led to a proportionate as well as absolute increase in the number of salaried local officers.

Yet even with the increase in the size of the union hierarchy, the number of opportunities for workers to rise from the ranks to significant union posts obviously is not very large. In relation to the number of workers who belong to the union, the number of salaried officials is comparatively small, probably not more than one to every 1,250 workers in 1951. Nor is there a rapid turnover among those who do hold office. International representatives, although without fixed tenure, usually possess considerable job security. Turnover among them is not high unless there is a major internal political upheaval such as occurred in 1947 (when, for example, all four international representatives in Autotown were replaced). As long as they do their work reasonably well and do not incur the antagonism of their superiors, who can recommend their dismissal to the International Executive Board, as long as there is no financial need to cut the size of the union staff, they can be reasonably sure of retaining their positions.

Since local officers are elected annually (the 1951 U.A.W. convention voted down a proposal for biennial local elections), personnel shifts are perhaps more likely to occur on the local than the international level. But even annual elections do not necessarily mean frequent changes. While four men held the presidency of the A.B.C. local from 1942 through 1951, only one worker served as financial secretary during that period. A relatively efficient local administration is not likely to be unseated easily. The "ins" usually have advantages over the "outs" in an election.

Despite the comparatively small number of salaried union offices and the slow rate of turnover among officeholders, the union remains a real alternative to the traditional avenues of advancement for at least a few men who might otherwise have had no chance to rise from the level of wage labor in the factory. And advancement in the union is open to everyone without regard to origins; it requires the initiative, drive, persistence, and ability defined by the tradition of opportunity as prerequisite for success, and does not demand any formal education or training. (It is possible, however, that those men who gain desirable jobs in the union hierarchy have had more education than the average worker.)

If there were wide competition for those positions that did become available, both in the locals and on the international staff, many workers would necessarily be subject to disappointment and frustration. But union office does not present itself to most workers as an avenue of individual mobility. The existence of an ideology of leadership which stresses personal sacrifice and disinterestedness functions as a strong check on active interest in union office; indeed, at times it acts so effectively that the union faces the problem of stimulating active participation among its members. Unlike business, which has traditionally viewed the common good as the unplanned product of the pursuit of naked self-interest, and unlike the professions, which assume that adherence to impersonal, universalistic standards of performance leads to personal success, union leadership carries with it an almost explicit assumption that private interest and group welfare necessarily conflict.

Leadership in the union has assumed a semisacred quality so that anyone who profanes his role by evidencing personal ambition is an object of strong disapproval. The motives typically attributed to union leaders by rank-and-file members are humanitarianism, a sense of justice, concern for others, or antagonism to management. The worst that can be said of a union leader or a candidate for office is that he is ambitious or an opportunist. Union leaders themselves usually give as their motives such reasons as: "I hate to see a fellow get kicked around and not get what's coming to him," "I like to see a fellow get what's coming to him, 'specially from management," or "I'm in this because I want to do a job for the union and I think I'm qualified to do it." The result of this semisacred quality of union leadership, in sociological terms, is that its mobility function in relation to the traditional values of success is latent rather than manifest. It occurs in spite of, rather than because of, the intentions of both organizers and members of the union.

This ideology of sacrifice and selflessness emerged during the years when automobile producers sought with every available means to stave off organization of their workers. Mere possession of a union card could lead to instant dismissal, persistent union activity to blacklisting. With the risks they took, union leaders were necessarily devoted to their cause, careless of self, and ready to make substantial sacrifices. They were stamped as rebels against the established order with little concern for the traditional values of personal success.

The circumstances which gave rise to the ideal of the selfless, devoted leader have largely disappeared; the personal risks to which organizers and active members were once exposed are virtually gone. Indeed, workers who assume a full-time union office usually do not even lose their seniority standing in the plants from which they come; they are given leave for the duration of their union assignment and can return to their previous jobs at any time. Further, though it would be easy to overstress the point, union officials have also gained some degree of recognition as community leaders through membership on welfare councils, school boards, and other public organizations. Nevertheless, the very nature of the union official's role and of the path to office in the union sustain the frequently expressed belief that "you've got to have it in your heart to do the job."

Full-time work for the union almost inevitably entails much more time than the eight hours each day put in by the ordinary factory worker. The union official must attend an almost endless procession of meetings of various sorts. The president of the A.B.C. local, for example, normally attends the monthly meetings of the local, the local executive board, the steward's council of the local, and the Autotown C.I.O. Council. He frequently attends the occasional meetings of workers from one or another district of the plant, of the various committees of the local, as well as occasional political caucuses. Nor is this a complete list. In addition, he may be called at any time by workers with problems or grievances.

So strenuous are the demands on union officials' time that they are likely to prevent the pursuit of personal interests. Painting one's house, digging in one's garden, or merely having a good time must be set aside or neglected. Even one's family may be neglected in favor of union meetings or other union responsibilities.* This inability to satisfy personal interests in a culture which emphasizes the personal and private rather than the social is widely looked upon as the sacrifice which union leaders must make. This sacrifice is to all intents and purposes directed to no personal ends; union officials have no direct personal interest in the goals toward which they direct their energies. They are continually giving up their time for the welfare of others. And local officers may even spend a good part of their time on problems which have nothing to do with work in the factory. In the course of his day the local union president may perform such varied services for members as arrange for a loan from a credit union or for some service from a social agency, help the worker secure compensation for an injury suffered on the job, or even resolve a family quarrel and give advice about buying a house. Two local presidents estimated that over half of their time was taken up with personal problems of workers rather than their job problems in the plant.

The ideology of selflessness gains further support from the fact that the path to union office usually begins in the local union with positions at the bottom of the hierarchy which are widely labeled as "thankless tasks." While a few men catapulted to the top in the first chaotic years of organization, the possibility of such meteoric progress now is slight. Only technically trained men needed for professional and semiprofessional tasks can now expect to move directly into the upper levels of the union bureaucracy without preliminary experience in lower positions in the hierarchy.† All of the six A.B.C. workers who held union office of any sort, including the editor of the Autotown C.I.O. weekly paper, as well as the other international representatives in the city, had begun as shop stewards or commit-

---

* A. W. Gouldner has shown clearly how family demands may conflict with the demands of union office, even among leaders who are dedicated to their cause and whose wives are in sympathy with their sentiments. "Attitudes of Progressive Trade Union Leaders," *Amer. J. Sociol.* 52:389–392 (March, 1947).

† The union even prefers, if at all possible, to choose for its technical staff men who not only possess the requisite training, but who also have worked in the factory and belong to the union. The editor of the Autotown C.I.O. weekly paper, for example, had been a newspaperman who had gone into the plant during the war and become active in the union, serving for a time as a steward.

teemen in the factory and had usually held other unsalaried local offices
too.

The most frequent starting place for a union career is a position as a shop
steward whose task is to settle the grievances of workers in the department or "district" of the plant which he represents. (Stewards in the A.B.C.
plant represented districts, each of which covered several departments.
Each district was designed so that it included approximately 250 workers.)
An article in the local labor paper entitled "What is a Steward?" concluded
with the summary statement: "He should have the patience of Job, the skin
of a rhinoceros, the cunning of a fox, the courage of a lion, be blind as a
bat and silent as a sphinx." On the one hand, the steward must cope with
the opposition of management. On the other, he is held responsible for
the successful prosecution of grievances. Failure to secure what an aggrieved
worker wants may elicit criticism and recriminations, despite the generally
recognized fact that not all grievances are justified and that not all justifi-
able grievances can be successfully settled. In addition, even the minor post
of a shop steward may draw the worker into the constant round of after-
work activities, particularly if he takes his responsibilities seriously.

Membership on the shop committee, the next step upward in the union
hierarchy, exposes the worker to even greater demands on his time and
presents him with greater problems. The shop committee (which numbered
seven in the A.B.C. plant) carries on the day-by-day negotiations with plant
management with regard to general shop issues and tries to settle those
grievances which the steward has not been able to resolve with the department foreman. Shop committeemen therefore necessarily deal with the
most difficult grievances from all parts of the plant, as well as with general shop problems. The demands on their time and energies are almost
as great as those made on salaried union officers.

Because of the ideology of sacrifice and these objective circumstances
which contribute to its persistence, few workers see in union office an opportunity for individual advancement, even though they can simultaneously
recognize the concrete advantages available to men who are willing to
make the necessary effort. While remaining staunchly loyal to the union,
most workers see in it primarily a collective instrument to which they pay
their dues, from which they gain protection against management and advancement of their economic group interests. They are willing to have
others derive such benefits as are available in return for looking after their
interests. A spokesman for a group of workers with a collective grievance
which the union had been unable to settle commented at a union meeting:
"I wouldn't be down here if things were running smoothly. I don't have
to spend an evening here if things are going all right."

Workers who do gain office and become part of the union bureaucracy may begin their careers, Mills has suggested, as "business-like men," as "political men," or as "disgruntled working men."[4] In addition, our data suggest, there are those whose initial step in the union is a response to the encouragement of others, rather than a product of ambition, ideology, or dissatisfaction. Except for the "business-like men," who are not numerous, most workers do not become active in the union with an eye to full-time union work. On the contrary, aspirations for salaried union office are more frequently the result of active participation than its cause.

It seems a tenable hypothesis, as Mills suggests,[5] that *a priori* calculation of career possibilities in the union occurs primarily among men who have had white-collar experience prior to becoming factory workers. The only case in which a union official admitted that he had become active in the union in hopes of eventually securing a salaried job in the organization was a former schoolteacher who had become a factory worker because of the high wages paid in the automobile industry.

> When the C.I.O. got started [he said] I asked somebody how I could get a job with them and he told me I had to start in the local union. So I got active in the local, got elected to a couple of offices, and finally got on the payroll.

The middle-class person is particularly likely to be aware of the prerogatives of union office; his usually greater education and a wider range of social skills fit him for a position of leadership and responsibility.

The "political men," guided by a more or less explicit ideology, become active in the union and seek office in order consciously and deliberately to utilize the union as an instrument of political and economic change. In the past, they derived their ideologies primarily from strong strains of liberal and radical thought which, though fed by European socialists, have had a long indigenous history in the United States. On the national level, the Reuther brothers provide outstanding examples of such political men. In Autotown, one local union president explained that socialist beliefs acquired from his father had, in part, stimulated him to participation in the union. But in the present, with the atrophy of some radical political ideologies and the decline of others, there are not likely to be many new political men entering union activities.

The "disgruntled working men," angered over some action by management, harboring some deep-seated resentment, or seeking a way out of economic difficulties, turn to the union as an instrument through which they can fight back. One member of the shop committee in the A.B.C. plant attributed his first venture into union affairs to a foreman who was a "slave driver." "I told him," he said, "that he made a good union man out of me." During the depression, many workers became active in the union because they saw in it an instrument through which they might deal with the problems they were facing.[6]

Finally, some workers were virtually pushed into office by their fellows. When, as occasionally happens, no one wants to run for office as a steward, some worker is informally chosen, his name put up, and his attempts to withdraw discouraged. As one steward explained, in words almost identical with those used by several others:

> They just elected me one day. I didn't want it, but the old steward dropped out and they needed somebody. I used to talk about the union and things with them and they just elected me.

This spontaneous choice is usually an informal group leader or spokesman for a group, someone who has shown some ability to express ideas, to argue effectively, and to assume responsibility. "The men are always looking for someone who has a definite opinion and offers leadership," said one union officer who had held one salaried position or another for ten years. Unless his personal objections are particularly strong, the worker who has achieved an informal position of leadership cannot avoid accepting the formal post as representative of his fellows.

In concrete cases, motives are usually mixed. As Mills points out, in each case it is a question of emphasis.[7] The ambitious middle-class man in the factory, for example, may justify his ambition in ideological terms. Indeed, with his middle-class values challenged by his objective working-class position, he is especially ready to adopt either a simple trade-union philosophy or a radical political ideology in which unionism plays an important part. But beneath the ideology the "little motors of ambition are laboring away." The disgruntled working man and the worker pushed into union office may similarly subscribe to a radical political ideology or may possess vague ideas concerning a union career. But whatever leads men to become stewards— ambition, informal leadership, dissatisfaction, ideology, or any combination of these—their experience in the union may serve both to stimulate their desire for higher positions and to provide the skills and knowledge requisite for advancement in the hierarchy.

Even as shop stewards at the bottom of the union hierarchy workers cannot help becoming aware of the concrete rewards to be gained in union office. They immediately derive some advantage from their own position: they are given top seniority status in their districts. According to the A.B.C. contract with the union, if ten men are working in a district, the steward or his alternate must be called in to work. If there is a layoff, the steward is the last in his district to be laid off. In addition, they can leave their usually routine jobs for two hours each day in order to handle grievances.

These rewards are even greater for workers on the shop committee. Each shop committeeman has top seniority in his zone (for purposes of dealing with grievances the plant is also divided into zones comprising several districts, in each of which a committeeman functions). Committeemen can leave their jobs for five hours each day for purposes of negotiation. And the chairman of the shop committee has top seniority in the plant and can leave his job at any time for as long as necessary in connection with union business.

The steward may also come to see that the ostensible liabilities of union office have compensating values. The dedication of time and effort usually defined as "sacrifice" involves the worker in a round of social activities and a network of social relationships which may be in themselves intrinsically satisfying. The more deeply involved a man is in union affairs, the more extended is his social participation. In an increasingly impersonal urban world, the union may come to serve as an institutional center where active participants can find companionship and sociability.

The extreme illustration of such circumstances was found in a member of the shop committee for whom the union had become the chief focus of his social existence. Divorced, in his late thirties, living alone in a furnished room, he had found that "I wouldn't know what to do with myself if there wasn't the union. I don't like to hang around beer parlors or anything like that. So I keep busy in the union during the week, except for Thursday when I like to go to the wrestling."

Some stewards find in negotiating and bargaining an unexpected source of personal gratification which stimulates their desire for continued and extended activity. One four-term local president observed: "There are some men who get into leadership because they like to bargain with management. It inflates their egos, sort of, and they get a kick out of it, and then they really get interested." A shop steward who was running for office as a member of the shop committee commented:

> I like to argue with the stuffed shirts there. Sometimes I show them that they're wrong. Sometimes I'm wrong. But we've always got squabbles. That's what's interesting in it.

In the bargaining situation, differences in status and power are to some extent dissipated. The shop steward is on a par with the foreman, the shop committeeman with top corporation executives.

Unlike most nonskilled factory jobs, the position of shop steward permits the worker to "grow, to develop his ability to make a greater contribution to the whole, and to improve his own position as well." If he is conscientious about his duties, the steward may learn a good deal about the union contract and the union machinery. Attendance at local meetings and at educational sessions designed particularly for stewards is strongly encouraged. His name is placed on the mailing list of the international union for literature aimed at thousands like himself. (In the A.B.C. local alone there were forty-four stewards and alternates.) He is encouraged to take courses sponsored by the union in public speaking, collective bargaining, economics, and labor history. If he is willing to accept additional responsibility, he may be placed on some committee where there is always room for a willing worker. On occasion, he may be sent to one of the conferences sponsored by the union or to one of the union's summer schools for a week's study, all at the union's expense, and with his regular factory wages paid as well. (For several years the U.A.W. has been operating twelve summer camps for its members in various parts of the country.)

In addition to the skills in bargaining and in parliamentary discussion and the modicum of organizational *savoir-faire* which he may thus acquire, the shop steward may also develop some capacity for political leadership and a following among the rank-and-file membership, both significant prerequisites for further advancement in the union. While the shop steward is chosen by the workers whom he represents, all higher officers in the local are elected by the entire membership,* and political support is even in many cases a necessary prerequisite for appointment to office in the union bureaucracy. Under some circumstances, the political prerequisites for appointment to the union staff may be of much greater importance than possession of the skills and knowledge relevant to the organizational and bargaining tasks to which international representatives and local officers may be assigned.

Membership on the shop committee, the next significant step in the union hierarchy, provides the rich measure of experience and responsibility necessary to round out the worker's union training. Other offices—vice-president, treasurer, trustee, member-at-large on the executive committee—entail lesser duties (all of which must be performed after the day's work in the factory), possess few prerogatives, and are tangential to the main line of advancement within the union. Indeed, many workers in the A.B.C. local held such offices while serving as stewards in their respective districts.

Although not a formal prerequisite for higher union office, membership on the shop committee seems to be a useful and frequent preliminary. In the several elections held by the A.B.C. local during the course of the investigation, all candidates for the two salaried offices had been or were at

---

* Locals which include workers from several factories or from sharply separated parts of one plant are frequently divided into "units" in an "amalgamated local." Each unit elects its own officers as well as voting for officers for the entire local.

the time members of the shop committee. All the international representatives in Autotown and those from the A.B.C. local who were serving elsewhere had also at some time been members of the shop committee in their respective plants.

Frequent meetings with top management in the plant provide committeemen with an opportunity to develop and demonstrate negotiating and bargaining skills. They necessarily deal with general issues as well as with specific grievances. They must frequently defend their actions before meetings of the union. They learn how to prepare briefs for presentation to the impartial umpire supported by the union and the Corporation. In the process of settling grievances, they may build up political support throughout the plant, for every worker whose grievance is settled to his satisfaction is a potential backer.

Out of this progressive experience in the local union may come aspirations for union office, for a career in the union. One local officer, commenting about himself and his colleagues, remarked:

> I think that everybody who gets active thinks that some day he might get a union job. Of all the people on the top committee, there's only one who probably doesn't think of it. I know I myself have thought of it. I've thought I might try to make a career out of working for the union. I could possibly get a job and then if I had the stuff I could probably stay. Most of them won't admit it, but they would like to be on the union payroll.

Some workers who hold office as stewards or committeemen for a year or for several years eventually find its demands upon their capacity too great or its gratifications inadequate to balance those things they have had to give up, and withdraw from active participation as officeholders. Others find satisfaction in their tasks in the local and seek to retain their office. But because they feel inadequate for higher office or are unwilling to assume greater responsibility, they do not seek advancement in the hierarchy. To these latter men who do what is widely called the "Jimmy Higgins work," the unrewarded chores without which the union could not continue to function effectively, the union becomes more than an institutional device for securing protection in the plant and for bettering their economic circumstances as a group. It also becomes the locus for a kind of personal and social experience they could not secure elsewhere.

The concrete rewards and gratifications derived from union office by both the ambitious and unambitious not only balance the difficulties and sacrifices which are required, they may also make the job in the factory seem much more satisfying and lead to diminished interest in out-of-the-shop goals. Energies which might be directed toward starting a small business are focussed instead upon the union, perhaps with an eye to eventual elec·

tion to a salaried office or appointment as a full-time staff member. Those who already hold full-time positions in the union are too fully occupied to look for other alternatives.

The advantages of union office may also, in part, lead workers to reject opportunities for promotion to foremanship. This rejection of a traditionally sanctioned step upward, however, is likely to be rationalized or justified in terms of loyalties to the union which are based upon more than economic self-interest. These loyalties are fostered to a substantial extent by the ideology of union leadership which was described earlier in this chapter. Acceptance of a position in management is likely to be thought of and described as a betrayal of a moral commitment to the organization and to one's fellow workers. (As relations between union and management become less tinged with conflict, however, those who do move into management from the union are less likely to be looked upon by those with strong union loyalties as renegades or traitors. Indeed, some union leaders may see the selection of active members for positions as foremen as an important step toward better day-by-day relations with management.)

Although union office is therefore objectively an alternative to traditional paths of advancement for some workers, it is not, in ideological or cultural terms, equivalent to foremanship or a successful small business as a way of getting ahead. Because they are committed to values which differ from those dominant in American society, workers who pursue union careers may secure the objective perquisites of higher status, but usually they cannot feel that they are really becoming successful.

Footnotes to Chapter VIII

1. C. W. Mills: *The New Men of Power*, New York, Harcourt, Brace & Co., 1948, pp. 107–108.
2. See Mills, *op. cit.*, *passim*, and the classic discussion in S. and B. Webb: *History of Trade Unionism*, New York, Longmans, Green, & Co., Inc., 1911, pp. 431–478.
3. From a statement by Emil Mazey, Secretary-Treasurer of the U.A.W.-C.I.O., *Proceedings of the Thirteenth Constitutional Convention of the United Automobile, Aircraft, and Agricultural Implement Workers of America (U.A.W.-C.I.O.)*, Cleveland, Ohio, April 1–6, 1951, p. 327.
4. Mills, *op. cit.*, p. 95.
5. *Ibid.*, pp. 95–96.
6. For an autobiographical account of how the depression stimulated union activity in a previously passive worker, see C. Fountain: *Union Guy*, New York, Viking Press, 1949, Chapters 1–6.
7. Mills, *op. cit.*, p. 96.

The Chronology of Aspirations

Despite the cultural admonition to pursue large ambitions, automobile workers, as we have seen, focus their aspirations on a narrow range of alternatives. They do not aspire to the top levels of business and industry; they want to become skilled workers, to gain promotion to supervision, to engage in small-scale farming, to open a retail store or a small service establishment of some kind. Since even most of these alternatives entail serious difficulties, however, comparatively few workers persist in hope, remain strong in intention, or persevere in effort. But desire frequently survives.

The varied patterns of desire, intention, plan, and effort revealed by the workers interviewed in Autotown must be seen as only in part the reactions of workers with different personal and social characteristics to similar concrete circumstances. To some extent, these varied patterns of aspirations with regard to both advancement in the plant and out-of-the-shop goals constitute a series linked in time; the same worker may change from one pattern to another as he moves through his occupational career. Indeed, the following hypotheses which have already emerged from our analysis suggest the existence of a more or less typical chronology of aspirations among these workers in a mass-production industry.

1. Many young men who come to work in the factory define their jobs as temporary; they do not expect to remain in the ranks of factory labor (p. 88).

2. Workers with the most clearly defined out-of-the-shop goals are married men in their late twenties or early thirties who have not acquired substantial seniority (p. 87).

3. Workers are most likely to develop or sustain hope for promotion to supervision if while still relatively young they gain some form of advancement as wage workers, that is, if they secure jobs at the top of the hierarchy of desirability or if they move from nonskilled to skilled work (p. 51).

4. The longer workers remain in the plant, the less likely are they to

muster the initiative to leave, even if they continually talk of doing so (pp. 92–93).

5. As their seniority increases, workers can look forward to the possibility of individual wage increases (however small they may be) and of transfer to more desirable jobs (pp. 39–40, 77–78).

6. The weight of increasing or already heavy family responsibilities keeps men with long seniority from seriously considering out-of-the-shop goals (p. 93).

7. Workers who do not gain promotion to supervision before the age of forty or thereabouts quickly lose hope because of management's preference for younger men (pp. 50–51).

8. After workers reach the low wage ceiling at the top of the hierarchy of desirability, they may be satisfied with what they have achieved or, alternatively, they may become bitter and frustrated because of their inability to go further (pp. 79–80).

9. Some workers, as they approach the age of retirement, may become interested in out-of-the-shop goals as sources of income for their remaining years (p. 84).

Only a careful longitudinal study could test these hypotheses and expose in full detail the changing patterns of workers' aspirations. But we can, on the basis of our data, fill in the broad outlines of the chronology of aspirations suggested by these hypotheses.*

From these propositions it seems clear that workers' aspirations emerge from a process in which hope and desire come to terms with the realities of working-class life. But this process is not one which sees simply the gradual dissolution of originally large expectations as obstacles to advancement become evident. Instead we find that workers must repeatedly accommodate new desires generated by fresh stimuli to the concrete circumstances they face at different stages of their occupational careers.

The changing patterns of workers' aspirations therefore bear little resemblance to the popular stereotype of single-minded striving toward ambitious goals. It may well be that the rational tradition in our culture has continually overplayed man's singleness of purpose, that, encouraged by the pioneer ethos of self-help, we have overstressed the power of individual effort against the press of circumstances. It is quite likely that finding oneself vocationally involves in most cases considerable floundering among

---

* Our data consist primarily of retrospective accounts and of comparisons of workers of different ages, supplemented by the material from the dozen workers who were interviewed more than once. Both types of data must, of course, be used with caution, and their inadequacies for constructing a chronological pattern taken into account. Retrospective accounts are likely to contain some distortion of past events and attitudes; age comparisons suffer from the changing historical contexts in which men of different generations grow up and pursue their occupational careers.

available alternatives, that few men exhibit the terrible tenacity of Henry Ford or the elder Rockefeller. It seems altogether possible that for men on the level of wage labor, the period of floundering lasts longer, perhaps indefinitely, as they pitch such ambitions as they muster against the limited opportunities available to them.

The process of reconciling desire with reality begins early for industrial workers. In the public schools, if not at home, the working-class youth is repeatedly exposed to the values of success, the belief in the existence of opportunity for all, and the varied prescriptions for getting on in the world. "We were talking about Abe Lincoln in school and how he worked himself up," said the eighteen-year-old son of a machine-operator who had performed the same kind of work in the factory for eighteen years. "That shows that working yourself up depends on the person, not on the chances you have." But as soon as he leaves school, or even before, the working-class youth must come to terms with a world of limited opportunity where there are few chances. Lacking financial resources, he cannot look forward to the possibility of professional training, or even to four years of college which would widen his perspectives and increase his skills. He cannot step into a family business or acquire easily the funds with which to launch one of his own. As soon as his education ends, he must find some kind of job. And in Autotown even a large proportion of high-school graduates will probably become factory workers; a third of all employed persons in the city were engaged in factory labor of some kind, primarily in the four large automobile plants.

Many working-class boys therefore give up dreams of a rich and exciting occupational future—if they ever have such dreams—even before taking their first full-time job. In a questionnaire submitted to all boys about to graduate from Autotown's two high schools in June, 1947 and June, 1948, the question was asked: "If you could do what you wanted to what occupation would you choose?" Forty per cent of all working-class boys (forty-seven of 118) had no choice or chose occupations which carried comparatively little prestige and provided only limited rewards. (Occupations included in those with low prestige and low rewards were skilled work, clerical jobs, military service, and miscellaneous jobs which required no training. Those with high prestige and high rewards were the professions, technical and semiprofessional occupations, art and literature, scientific farming, and business.) Only twenty-three per cent of the middle-class boys, on the other hand, were without a choice or chose low-prestige, low-reward occupations, indicating a statistically significant difference.* When asked about their

---

* A. B. Hollingshead reports similar findings in his discussion of class differences in the levels of aspiration among teen-age youth. See *Elmtown's Youth*, New York, John Wiley

actual intentions, forty per cent of the working-class boys said that they merely intended to "look for a job," without specifying any particular kind of job. Another twenty per cent intended to learn a skilled trade, to apply for some definite manual job which did not require previous training, or to enlist in the armed services. These figures compare with fifteen and twelve per cent respectively for boys of middle-class origin.

Some working-class boys, particularly those without academic aptitudes or interests, may quit school as soon as they are able to secure a job since they feel that they will find themselves in the factory eventually, even if they do graduate from high school. They can no longer do as their parents might have done in the past, leave school in order to learn a trade, since admission to formal apprentice training for any trade now usually requires a high-school diploma. The jobs they find, therefore, promise little for the future.

Many working-class boys only come to grips with vocational reality when they finally graduate from high school. Stimulated to a high level of aspiration by the mass media, encouraged by parents and, sometimes, by teachers, they entertain inflated ambitions until the time when they must choose a definite course of action. For example, a third of the boys whose parents were manual workers reported that they intended to go to college. While some boys with requisite academic abilities do muster the necessary financial resources and enter college, most of them in fact find themselves looking for a job after they graduate from high school. According to high-school officials, less than a third of all graduates from Autotown's two high schools go to college, most of them probably from middle-class families. An even smaller proportion ever complete work for a degree. It is therefore highly probable that a very large proportion of those working-class boys who said that they intended to go to college did not do so.

The quick surrender by working-class youth to the difficulties they face is not necessarily forced or unwilling. Although they are encouraged to focus their aspirations into a long future and to make present sacrifices for the sake of eventual rewards, they are chiefly concerned with immediate gratifications. They may verbally profess to be concerned with occupational success and advancement (as did fourteen working-class boys who were interviewed), but they are likely to be more interested in "having a good time" or "having fun." They want to "go out," to have girl friends, to travel, to own a car or a motorcycle. When asked if "fun" would be given up in order

& Sons, Inc., 1949, pp. 282–287. Most studies of job choice among high-school students have stressed the generally inflated character of youthful aspirations and the inevitable comedown rather than noting the differences in the extent to which students from different classes respond to the American Dream. See, for example, D. S. Miller and W. H. Form: *Industrial Sociology*, New York, Harper and Brothers, 1951, pp. 589–592.

to take a job which might lead to advancement in the future, an eighteen-year-old boy about to graduate from high school answered: "Do you want me to tell you the truth? I'd rather have fun."

The concern with immediate gratifications unrelated to one's occupation is encouraged by prevalent values in American society. The massed apparatus of commercial advertising incessantly stimulates the desire for things which are immediately available—on the installment plan, if necessary. Together with movies, television, radio, and magazines, advertising sets up attractive—and expensive—models of leisure and recreation. And these models have become increasingly important as American culture has shifted from a central concern with the values of production to the values of consumption.[1] In a long-range sense, the pecuniary animus of the culture back-fires among working-class youth, for the desire for maximum income, when linked with an emphasis upon immediate satisfactions in the sphere of consumption, leads to decisions which virtually eliminate the possibility of a steadily increasing income in the future. "Sometimes I say to myself," said a thirty-year-old machine-operator who could have attended college but had instead gone to work in the factory, ". . . you could have been somebody . . . if you hadn't been so interested in the almighty dollar."

Since "fun" in this world of commercialized entertainment requires money, the immediate objective becomes a well-paid job, a goal most easily achieved by going to work in an automobile plant. Within a few months the son of an automobile worker who goes to work in the factory may be earning as much as his father, who may have been there for twenty years. Despite the low status of factory work and the hope frequently expressed by automobile workers that their sons will not follow in their steps, many boys head for factory personnel offices as soon as they are old enough or as soon as they finish high school. And others find themselves seeking factory employment after having tried other, less remunerative jobs.

Many of these young workers are aware of the dead-end character of most factory jobs. "You don't get advanced by going in the factory; there's no future there," said one high-school senior whose father had spent his entire adult life in the city's automobile factories. When they do go into the factory, they therefore define their jobs as temporary, particularly if they have earned a high-school diploma. They say that they intend to stay in the factory only until a promising opportunity comes along. In this fashion they can maintain the impression, both for themselves and for others, that they still intend to get ahead, that they are still ambitious.

Because the first job is frequently on the assembly line, these young workers do not quickly become satisfied. They soon seek ways of gaining a more desirable job in the factory. But beyond that limited goal they pay little attention to the possibilities of advancement. They are too young to expect promotion to supervision. They are unwilling to undertake apprentice training, in part because they would have to accept lower wages temporarily, in part because they may not possess the necessary aptitudes or education, in part because they may define factory work itself as temporary.

Even if these young workers say that they intend, eventually, to "go into business," they make no definite plans. Their main interests lie in the things they do in their leisure hours. For example, a twenty-two-year-old single worker in the plant cared little for his work, although he boasted that he had managed to secure a transfer from the assembly line to a job which consisted of driving completed cars off the end of the line. He had gained this transfer by threatening to quit in a period of acute labor shortage. (Since he had no family responsibilities, he probably would have quit and gone to work in some other factory if he had not been transferred.) He had not thought of the possibility of foremanship or of learning a trade. He insisted, however, that he would some day leave the factory—"I don't intend to stay here forever," he said—but he had no concrete objectives or plans. His chief interests were baseball, girls, and his car. He had recently bought a new A.B.C. car, but he wanted to replace it with the model which was scheduled to appear at the beginning of the following year. One reason for going to work in the A.B.C. plant rather than elsewhere was the fact that A.B.C. employees with more than six months seniority were given a large discount if they bought a new car.

Several older workers gave retrospective accounts of similar behavior which had preceded their "settling down." A forty-year-old union officer commented:

> Most young fellows are just like I was, they can't see ahead of their noses. They just want to have a good time and the devil take the rest of it. If they can make more money that's where they'll go. They don't think about anything else.

"Before I got married," said a thirty-nine-year-old oiler (whose work consisted of oiling moving parts of large machines, a nonskilled job), "I was only interested in three things, getting paid on Saturday, getting drunk on Saturday night, and having a girl." Others are undoubtedly more sober and conservative in their interests, but their attitudes toward their work and their future are much the same: as long as the pay is good and the job not too demanding or difficult, they are content to go along from day to day seeking their pleasures in leisure hours, careless about the future.

It seems a tenable hypothesis that this pattern of youthful aspirations represents a modal type which applies to a substantial proportion of working-class youth, as well as those lower-middle-class boys who become non-skilled factory workers. The chief deviation from this pattern is the youth who decides early to become a skilled worker, or who decides after a short tenure in the factory to apply for apprentice training. His ambitions do not focus on rich images of success, but on the promise of a reasonable income, a respected status in the community, and a job which provides interesting work.

These latter values conflict, however, with the immediate gratifications which can be gained by going to work in the factory as a nonskilled laborer. The teen-age working-class youth is not likely to make the sacrifice of present satisfactions unless his aspirations gain support from a personally significant model or are encouraged by persons whom he respects, admires, or loves. One thirty-one-year-old skilled worker whose father had also been a skilled worker commented:

> When I was an apprentice I was torn by two desires. One was to go to work on the line like the rest of my friends and make some money. But there's no future in that. The other was to stick to the apprenticeship in hopes of getting some place. Seeing the way my dad worked through—even if he had his troubles and lost his home—I felt that it paid my father dividends anyway.

It is noteworthy that thirty-nine per cent of all apprentices registered with the Autotown Technical School in 1947* (fifty of 129) were sons of skilled workers; only eleven per cent were the sons of nonskilled workers. The rest came from the urban lower-middle class or from farm families.

The typical attitudes of young nonskilled workers toward jobs, advancement, and the future persist until marriage or, perhaps, parenthood. With the assumption of family responsibilities, workers tend to become actively concerned about the possibilities of advancement. "When I got married," said the oiler quoted above, "I suddenly realized that I'd better do something or I was really going to be stuck." The immediate need for more money leads workers to consider seriously the alternatives open to them and the arrival of children generates a fresh interest in the future.

By the time these workers marry and have children, however, they have already made decisions which limit the alternatives open to them. Some left high school in order to take jobs which offered little prospect of advancement; others went willingly into an automobile plant after graduating. Now they find that they lack the training which is requisite for advancement in the corporate hierarchy. They have gained no skills which can be used outside the factory. They have not added to their scanty knowledge about the

---

* This includes all apprentices in the city except those in the A.B.C. apprentice program. The A.B.C. plant provided its own classroom instruction for apprentices; all other apprentices received their classroom instruction at the Autotown Technical School.

prerequisites and potentialities of alternative jobs. Nor, in their concern with buying a car or having a good time, have they tried to acquire the resources which might enable them to buy a profitable farm or start a successful business.

The responsibilities of marriage and the uncertainties facing the non-skilled worker tend to keep attention focussed on the present and to counterbalance the new stimuli to planning for the future. The pressure of the weekly grocery bill, the rent or mortgage payment, installments on a refrigerator or a washing machine or vacuum cleaner, the need for a new pair of work pants or a pair of shoes for a child, the doctor's bill for a tonsil-lectomy, all keep life on a pay-day-to-pay-day basis. The future, for men in an industry known for irregular employment, bristles with threats. They are not usually well prepared to cope with unemployment or with sickness and accident, the normal hazards of life. And the future is still resonant with echoes of the depression of the 1930s; men were employed by the W.P.A. in Autotown until the eve of war in 1941. Workers may conclude, therefore, that "it doesn't pay to think about the future," as a thirty-one-year-old line-tender put it.

As unmarried men without responsibility, these workers were careless about the future; now they are forced into taking a defensive stance toward the future despite the stimulus to aspiration and effort. There is no change, therefore, in the pattern of life to which they have been accustomed; life's rhythms of tension and release remain short, from week-end to week-end, from one good time to another. Life may occasionally be pointed toward a vacation a few months ahead, toward Christmas or Easter, toward a birth-day or some other family celebration. But long-run desires and expectations are avoided as both past and future are minimized and life is compressed into the week's routine.

Lacking occupational skills and financial resources, most workers confine their aspirations to the limited array of alternatives we have already ex-amined. Since they are unwilling or unable to plan for the long future, they see these goals as isolated small moves rather than as part of a long-range plan. Only one worker, a would-be businessman, talked of becoming rich. He was a twenty-nine-year-old toolmaker who was about to open his own tool-and-die shop. Only the two young workers who intended to go to col-lege could see in their plans the beginning of a career. Unlike the profes-sional or the salaried officeholder, the factory worker does not see his present job as part of a career pattern which channels his aspirations and sustains his hope. Unlike the businessman, he has no ever-beckoning goal of increasing sales and expanding profits to stimulate his efforts.

Hope for one or another of the alternatives on which workers do focus their aspirations may, for a while, run high. Despite the obstacles in their path, some workers are determined and purposeful. The period shortly after marriage when workers become concerned with their future, when they are at or near their physical peak, when family responsibilities may still serve as a stimulant to ambition and effort rather than as a brake, is probably the time of maximum ambition and of greatest expectation, for skilled as well as nonskilled workers. As we have seen, four of the six workers who thought they might be chosen as foremen were about thirty years old and five of the eight who had taken positive steps toward out-of-the-shop goals were in their twenties or early thirties. (Two of these eight, it will be remembered, were over sixty years of age and were chiefly concerned with gaining a secure income for their remaining years.)

But many workers see little reason for hope when they assay the possibilities of advancement in the factory and examine the problems and the risks inherent in business or farming. If they have not already gained some advancement on the level of wage labor, they are not likely to see any prospect of promotion to supervision. Indeed, if they have not had an opportunity to learn how to carry responsibility and exercise authority, they are not likely, even if offered promotion, to be willing to take on the problems which they know are inherent in the foreman's role. In order to start a business or buy a farm, one needs money; the family responsibilities which stimulate ambition also make it difficult to save. If they do manage to start a business or buy a farm, not only must they risk their savings, they must also surrender whatever security their seniority in the plant gives them. (One might therefore expect that workers most intent on leaving the factory would be those who, for one reason or another, have not been in the plant for very long. Five of the eight workers with definite out-of-the-shop plans had been there for less than a year.)

Workers who feel impelled to seek advancement despite the limited opportunities in the factory and the risks inherent in leaving tend to dilute their aspirations to a loose welter of hopes and a medley of alternative plans. And workers whose insistent hopes and positive efforts do not bear quick fruit give up their ambitions after a while and cast about as vaguely and uncertainly as the others. Without a "life-plan" which commits them to follow a series of more or less recognized steps,[2] workers simultaneously entertain alternative goals, or they continually shift their attention from one goal to another, usually without investing much hope or effort in any particular one.

While waiting for advancement in the factory which may not come and, in any case, is largely contingent upon forces over which they have little or no control, workers frequently consider the possibility of going into business or buying a farm, as twenty-three of the sixty-two workers interviewed were doing. Even those who are hopeful about advancement in the plant recognize the uncertainties involved and may therefore look elsewhere at the same time. Thus four of the six workers who felt that they would eventually become foremen had also thought of leaving the factory and said that they planned to "go into business" if they did not gain the desired promotion within some reasonable time. (None had been promoted and all were still in the plant in June, 1951.)

Interest in out-of-the-shop goals usually represents, as suggested earlier,* the desire for escape from the factory rather than a positive search for success. Such interest is, therefore, particularly susceptible to changes in workers' job status and the conditions of work. These changes bear no positive relationship to the objective possibilities of success or failure in business or farming or to the nature of workers' resources or skills. Interest and, in some cases, action may therefore be stimulated—or inhibited—at the wrong time.

Thus business and farming ambitions are frequently whipsawed by changes in general business conditions. In the upward phase of the business cycle, when production is being maintained at a high level or is increasing and workers are regularly employed, the desire to leave the factory is at a minimum even though opportunities for small business may be at their best. When production falls off and temporary layoffs and short workweeks occur, interest in out-of-the-shop goals increases even though workers' resources are being rapidly drained away and the chances of business failure are especially high.

Interest in out-of-the-shop goals, as well as hope for advancement in the factory, may also fluctuate with variations in workers' feelings that occur without reference to changes in their jobs. For example, a welder, when first interviewed, complained about the difficulties in his job and was anxious to leave the factory despite his lack of savings and the importance he attached to his twelve years of seniority. He had been working on the second shift (4:00 P.M. to 12:30 A.M.) when interviewed and was obviously tired and irritable. When interviewed again several weeks later, he was on the first shift (workers in most departments changed shifts every four weeks), rested, and in much better spirits. He no longer complained about his job, and though he still talked about leaving the factory "some day," he did so without force or urgency.

In a moment of hope, stimulated by some unexpected suggestion, workers may undertake a correspondence course in salesmanship, in automobile repairing, in accounting, in foremanship. (Four workers volunteered the in-

---

* See Chapter VII.

formation that they had once taken some kind of correspondence course; two others were doing so at the time they were interviewed.) In a moment of discouragement, the course is dropped, the money invested in it lost completely. The tentative and uncertain character of such efforts was evident in the case of one worker who quickly asked the interviewer if he thought there was much value in the correspondence course in foremanship and supervision he was taking at the cost of $120. Two months later he dropped the course because he was not "getting anything out of it." At a time when things in the factory seem to be at their worst, workers may look into farm prices, search for a small business of some kind, perhaps answer advertisements for salesmen or look for other factory jobs. But as their mood changes, the search is ended, negotiations that may have been begun are broken off, workers fail to follow up the steps they have already taken.

It seems likely that interest in out-of-the-shop goals may be endlessly renewed by the constant turnover among workers, some of whom do go into business, farming, or white-collar jobs. (The weekly newspaper published by the Autotown C.I.O. Council frequently featured stories about union members who had gone into business for themselves.) But interest, when unsupported by knowledge or resources, rarely remains focussed on one particular objective for very long. Since many workers plan to do "something" "as soon as things get better," "if I can save up a few hundred dollars," or "when I get straightened out," they entertain in usually disorderly succession various out-of-the-shop goals which are critically scrutinized and rejected as impractical or are mulled over, dreamed about, vaguely examined, and eventually permitted to fade away. This pattern emerged clearly in the case of one worker who was interviewed three times. In the first interview he said that he was thinking of "buying some tourist property up north." When asked how much money he would need and how much he had, he admitted that he did not know how much he would need, had no savings, and did not expect to save any money within the near future. A month later he was talking of a turkey farm, again with little attention to the concrete problems he would face. A year later he said that he had been thinking of a "bee farm," but that he had finally given up any thought of leaving the plant.

The pattern of shifting goals and tentative plans may persist for the major part of a worker's occupational life. Occasionally plans congeal into positive action under the impact of a particularly strong stimulus or under the cumulative pressure of a series of events. Frequently these actions are abortive. Thus a thirty-one-year-old worker with twelve years of seniority who had been moved after the war from a job as a toolmaker-upgrader to an unskilled maintenance job to the paint line angrily left the factory in order to take a job in a small chemical plant in which his father worked, even though this move meant lower wages. Two years later he was back in the A.B.C. plant as a machine-operator, but now without the long seniority he had once had. A bitter disagreement with the foreman, an unresolved grievance, a job assignment to which he objects, these and many other specific occurrences can provoke a worker into quitting, even though he must start looking for another job without much likelihood of gaining any basic improvement. He may, as many have done, find himself back eventually at the same kind of work in the same plant.

The longer workers remain in the plant, the less seriously do they consider the possibility of leaving, even though they recognize that they are probably going to remain on the level of wage labor in the factory. Eventually they cease to entertain out-of-the-shop goals, accept the fact that they will remain in the factory, and confine their aspirations to a better job in the plant. This shift does not occur at any particular age; it may take place when a worker is thirty, it may not occur until he is fifty or even older. In some instances, of course, it may never occur. And a last burst of interest in business may appear as workers approach the age of retirement when, bedeviled by the economic problems of old age, they seek methods of supplementing whatever pension they are entitled to.

Workers give up their desire to leave the factory as they come to realize that they are not likely to be successful in business or farming and are not likely to gain much merely by changing jobs. At the same time they come to place a heavy stress upon the security provided by long seniority in the plant. This disappearance of ambition does not necessarily mean disappointment or frustration, however. Skilled workers, for example, may never consider any other alternative to their factory jobs, although many do in as amorphous a manner as do most nonskilled workers. They can count on a comparatively good income with a measure of security from a relatively interesting and satisfying job. The worker who manages to become skilled through some sort of upgrading program, formal or informal, may give up his out-of-the-shop goals and resign himself contentedly to what he has achieved. One worker, for example, was intent on buying a farm when he was interviewed in 1947. But in 1951, after he had been recalled to the electrician's job he had held as an upgrader during the war, he was no longer thinking of leaving the factory. Even nonskilled workers who manage to secure jobs at the top of the informal hierarchy of desirability may be reasonably satisfied, particularly if their ambitions were not set very high at the outset, if they have not felt pressure from their families to go into business or see a better job elsewhere, or if they have not been stimulated by the example of friends or relatives who have done well economically.

Some workers, scarred by experience, resign themselves to a future in the factory without satisfaction, but without resentment. They no longer demand much of life except for some kind of job and some assurance that they can keep it. One fifty-two-year-old line-tender, for example, had not held a regular job from 1932 until 1941; he had tried subsistence farming, small businesses of various kinds, and had worked at a wide variety of manual jobs. Now he was grateful to have a job, although he did not like assembly-line work, and he was hoping to be permitted to remain in the factory without being disturbed or forced to look for work again.

But if workers come to feel that they must stay in the factory because there is no opportunity in business or farming, if they do not have desirable jobs in the plant, if they began their careers with large ambitions and high hopes, or if they have seen relatives or friends "get ahead in the world," then their acceptance of a future in the factory is accompanied by bitterness and resentment aimed at themselves, at others, or at the world in general.

Footnotes to Chapter IX

1. See D. Riesman: *The Lonely Crowd*, and L. Lowenthal: "Biographies in Popular Magazines," in P. F. Lazarsfeld and F. Stanton, Eds.: *Radio Research, 1942–1943*, New York, Duell, Sloan and Pearce, 1944, pp. 507–520.
2. See K. Mannheim: *Man and Society in an Age of Reconstruction*, New York, Harcourt, Brace & Co., 1944, p. 56, 104n.

X

Aspirations and the Tradition of Opportunity

The tradition of opportunity imposes heavy burdens upon workers who must repeatedly reconcile desire, stimulated from diverse sources, with the realities of working-class life. Since each individual is assigned full responsibility for his economic fate, failure can be due only to limited ability or defects in character—lack of ambition or determination or initiative, for example—and not to the absence of opportunity. Self-regard and self-esteem are challenged by this assumption that failure to rise from the level of wage labor is "one's own fault." Since large ambitions and unremitting persistence are sanctioned not only as prerequisites for success, but also as intrinsically desirable traits whose absence testifies to a lamentable weakness of character, feelings of guilt may also be generated when men cease to strive for the rich rewards ostensibly available to all.

As we have noted earlier, workers may try to maintain the illusion of persisting ambition by defining their jobs in the factory as "temporary" and by incessantly talking of their out-of-the-shop goals and expectations. As long as workers can sustain this illusion, they can escape from the problems of self-justification created by their inability to rise and their low level of aspiration. But these expedients are themselves at best temporary, at worst only a public demonstration that one is ambitious—which may convince others* without assuaging inner feelings of guilt and self-blame. No matter what public image of plans and prospects workers can create, they still live in a world in which they have manifestly gained no substantial advancement. Eventually they may have to face up to the fact that they are likely to remain factory workers for the rest of their lives.

Since men do not readily reveal self-doubt and self-blame, it is difficult

---

* That talk of out-of-the-shop goals may not convince others on occasion is evident from our earlier discussion of farm ambitions. See pp. 91–92. And if one does not convince others that one actually intends to do something about these goals and that they are practical goals, it is not likely that one's talk will convince oneself either.

to gauge the extent to which workers find the reasons for their failure to rise out of the ranks of factory labor in their own actions, habits, or personality. Occasionally some of the men interviewed did give evidence of self-depreciation, guilt, and lowered self-regard. "I guess I'm just not smart enough," said a thirty-eight-year-old machine-operator who had never worked at anything except a factory job, laughing gently at himself as if to ease this self-evaluation. A thirty-two-year-old worker in parts and service who had never been employed anywhere except in the A.B.C. plant commented:

> It's my own fault. I was going to work here for a year after I graduated from high school and then be a printer's apprentice. But then I bought a car and that was my downfall. I couldn't afford to leave if I was going to have the car. Then I got married—and I certainly couldn't afford to quit.

And a thirty-year-old machine-operator who had also gone directly into the A.B.C. plant from high school exclaimed bitterly:

> Sometimes I look at myself in the mirror and I say to myself, Pat, you dumb so-and-so, you could have been somebody if you'd only set your mind to it and not been so interested in the almighty dollar.

(Pat could have gone to college with the assistance of a well-to-do relative, but had instead gone to work in the factory where he could earn high wages immediately.)

But most workers, it appears, frequently try to rationalize their status as factory employees and to justify their small ambitions. Despite the fact that their aspirations are controlled by a relatively objective appraisal of what is possible rather than by the unreliable image of America projected by the tradition of opportunity, most workers do not explain their failure to rise in terms of forces beyond their control. Nor do they feel that under the circumstances they could not be expected to pursue larger goals. Instead they try to maintain their self-regard by redefining advancement to include the goals and interests with which they are actively concerned, by projecting their hopes and aspirations upon their children, and, to a lesser extent, by minimizing success and emphasizing alternative values.

In order to convince themselves that they are getting ahead and that they are not without ambition, workers apply to the ends they pursue the vocabulary of the tradition of opportunity. They extend the meaning of ambition and advancement to include the search for security, the pursuit of small goals in the factory, and the constant accumulation of personal possessions.

Security, it has been frequently asserted, is replacing advancement as the major objective of most industrial workers. It seems highly probable that the automobile workers studied in this investigation *are* actually more interested in security than in traditional patterns of advancement. Workers' attitudes toward specific aspects of their job world reveal clearly their intense concern with security. They value a steady job over one that is not steady, even if the latter pays higher wages. They are unwilling to assume the risks inherent in small business despite their desire to leave the factory and be independent. They want to save as much as they can, not in order to be able eventually to strike out for themselves, but to provide protection against a "rainy day." They place great emphasis upon seniority, with its protection against arbitrary layoffs and its assurance of recall if one is laid off temporarily. The union's fight for a company pension plan drew strong support from these men because it articulated deep-seated concerns. And it seems likely that the union's increasing interest in the guaranteed annual wage will elicit a similar response.

But workers do not see security, thus concretely exemplified, as an alternative to advancement. Questions which were designed to elicit the relative importance assigned to security and opportunities for advancement frequently proved meaningless; the respondents could see no difference between them. "If you've got security, if you've got something you can fall back on, you're still getting ahead," said a twenty-eight-year-old truck-driver with three children. "If you can put away a couple of hundred dollars so you can take care of an emergency, then you're getting ahead," declared a forty-year-old nonskilled maintenance worker with four children. "If you work during a layoff, like back in the depression, that's my idea of working up," commented a thirty-two-year-old fender-wrapper who had been in the plant since 1935. And a thirty-nine-year-old oiler summed it up: "If you're secure, then you're getting ahead."

The small goals workers pursue in the factory resemble the prevailing cultural definition of advancement only in the case of small wage increases gained individually through promotion (although usually on the basis of the seniority rule). The more significant wage increases are now secured collectively through the union. And the other goals in the factory embody hitherto distinct values which are now assimilated to the idea of advancement. "Getting ahead," explained a machine-operator with ten years of seniority, "is working up to a job where you don't get kicked around." "I'll be getting ahead all right," declared a discontented line-tender, "if I can just get off the line." Upward movement in the informal hierarchy described in Chapter VI is equated with advancement even though it may mean no economic gain, no greater demands on skill, and no increase in responsibility.

In their efforts to reconcile their own ambitions and achievements with the tradition of opportunity, workers have also transformed what was once a symbol of economic success into a significant form of personal progress in itself. Advancement has come to mean the progressive accumulation of things as well as the increasing capacity to consume. A nonskilled maintenance worker who had been in the plant for fourteen years commented:

> A lot of people think getting ahead means getting to be a millionaire. Not for me though. If I can just increase the value of my possessions as the years go by instead of just breaking even or falling behind and losing, if I can keep adding possessions and property—personal property too—and put some money away for when I can't work, if I happen to own two or three houses like this one [which had cost $1,600 in 1940, of which he still owed eight hundred dollars] and have five thousand dollars put away in the bank, I'll figure I got ahead quite a lot.

The achievement which most clearly betokens advancement by purchase is home ownership, a goal already sanctioned and supported by a complex set of values. A thirty-nine-year-old welder living in one of the city's two slum areas remarked:

> We're all working for one purpose, to get ahead. I don't think a person should be satisfied. My next step is a nice little modern house of my own. That's what I mean by bettering yourself—or getting ahead.

If one manages to buy a new car, if each year sees a major addition to the household—a washing machine, a refrigerator, a new living-room suite, now probably a television set—then one is also getting ahead.

American culture encourages men to seek both occupational advancement and the acquisition of material possessions. But workers who respond to both of these admonitions use the second to rationalize their failure to achieve the first. As long as possessions continue to pile up, the worker can feel that he is moving forward; as long as his wants do not give out, he can feel that he is ambitious.

Workers may also attempt to cushion the impact of failure and to maintain an identification with the tradition of opportunity by projecting their unfulfilled ambitions upon their children—their extended ego, as it were. The hope that one's child may succeed where one has failed may make that personal failure seem less important; ambition for a child may substitute for ambition for oneself. "What sustains us as a nation," wrote Eleanor Roosevelt in one of her daily columns, "[is] the feeling that if you are poor you still see visions of your children having the opportunities you missed." Further, as we have already seen, the burden of family responsibilities, which includes concern for the future of one's children, serves as an acceptable justification for remaining in the factory rather than risking savings and security in business.

Sons of twenty-eight of the workers interviewed were not yet old enough to work. Among the fathers there was an almost universally expressed desire that their sons not go into the factory, that they "do better than that." The occasional intensity of this desire is suggested by the assertion of a forty-year-old line repairman whose sixteen-year-old son was talking of dropping out of high school: "If he goes into the factory I'll beat the hell out of him—except if he just goes in for a visit or if he goes to engineering school or learns a trade first."

Since most workers felt that they could not and should not dictate their children's occupational choices, their positive aspirations usually focussed upon education rather than upon specific occupations or professions, although a few did have definite occupational hopes—doctor, musician, artist, engineer. Thirteen of these twenty-eight workers hoped that their sons would go to college, seven wished that they would at least secure some kind of technical training after graduating from high school, and three merely insisted that their children should finish high school. The remaining five did not have any positive desires or hopes for their children.

The significance of these aspirations for children as a possible substitute for personal achievement emerged in the comment of a thirty-two-year-old machine-operator who had taken his first job in the depths of the Great Depression: "I never had a chance, but I want my kids to go to college and do something better than factory work." The direct relationship which may exist between the hopes men have for their children and their own unfulfilled interests and desires is suggested by a worker who, having once played an instrument in a high-school band, hoped that his son might become a professional musician, and by the would-be cartoonist who hoped that his four-year-old son would become an artist—seeing in his childish scribbling signs of some artistic capacity and interest.

Finally, workers may try to protect themselves from guilt and self-blame by stressing other values as substitutes for success, minimizing the importance of wealth. In a few instances, for example, workers asserted that what mattered was "happiness—and you don't need a lot of money for that," that what counted was "the kind of person you are and not how much money you have." Such assertions do not represent a radical rejection of American values. The importance of moral integrity, the happiness to be found in humble surroundings, the spuriousness of the single-minded search for fortune when human values are neglected are all familiar, though usually minor, themes in American culture. In emphasizing these themes, workers have not denied the desirability of economic success, but have sought to relegate it to a lesser position in the hierarchy of values.

Only in the occasional instances of men who could be defined in Marx's terms as *lumpenproletariat* or in W. L. Warner's terms as "lower-lower class" could one find workers who had totally rejected American success values. (No such workers were interviewed, although several were pointed out or identified.) But this solution to the problems imposed on workers by the disparity between their goals and achievements on the one hand and the tradition of opportunity on the other was in effect no solution. Such men offered no alternative values to replace those which they had rejected; they were in a state of anomy.

The efficiency with which these defensive rationalizations protect workers from the cultural attack upon the stability and integrity of their personalities is, of course, difficult to appraise. It does seem unlikely that they can be totally effective. In the immediate context of the factory and of a working-class community, small gains in the factory and security may represent important achievements. But when men move into a larger social context these gains may seem insignificant, and men are forced again to face the fact that they have not been able to get on in the world. In a society which emphasizes economic achievement as strongly as ours, it seems unlikely that workers can get away with their deprecation of success values. Indeed, the few men who tried to minimize the importance of economic achievement and to stress other values also felt it necessary to defend themselves in other ways which did not deny the importance of success.

There are serious and more obvious limits on the long-run efficacy of aspirations for children as a protection against the impact of failure. Lacking knowledge of occupational alternatives and possessing few resources with which to aid their children financially, most workers can only encourage and exhort, they cannot offer effective guidance or practical assistance. If their sons finally become factory workers, as a substantial proportion usually do,* not only must they surrender whatever ego-protection they have derived from their hopes, they may also be forced to bear a new burden: a sense of responsibility for their children's failure stemming from their own inability to provide guidance or assistance.

Workers can only succeed in the acquisition of possessions, even if they do not suffer from recurrent hard times, if they have mastered what Wesley

---

* There were nine adults among the male children of the workers interviewed. Four of these held nonskilled factory jobs. Two held minor white-collar jobs which might eventually be exchanged for factory work because of the low wages they paid. One was completing an apprentice course as a pattern-maker. One was studying engineering at the state university located nearby. One, the son of a skilled worker and grandson of a doctor, was a commercial photographer. In their study of occupational mobility in San Jose, California, P. E. Davidson and H. D. Anderson found that 58.2% of the sons of unskilled workers and 43.4% of the sons of semiskilled workers became either unskilled or semiskilled workers, as did 23.4% of the sons of skilled workers. *Occupational Mobility in an American Community*, Stanford University, Stanford University Press, 1937, p. 20, Table 4. These figures are comparable to those reported in other studies.

Mitchell once called "the backward art of spending money."[2] That they, together with most Americans, may not yet have mastered that art is suggested, for example, by John Dean's analysis of the risks inherent in buying a house. Ignorant of many of the problems of home ownership and unprotected against error and exploitation by institutional safeguards, workers—and others—may be defenseless against the "organized pressure to buy."[3]

Since these defensive measures are only partially effective, it seems probable that there remains among these workers a deep and substantial undercurrent of guilt and self-depreciation. The inability and failure to live up to the demands of the tradition of opportunity generate a process of self-justification in which frustration, guilt, and defensive rationalization follow one another in disorderly, almost endless, sometimes painful succession.

Both self-blame and the defensive rationalizations against self-blame, however, contribute to the maintenance of both existing economic institutions and the tradition of opportunity itself. To the extent that workers focus blame for their failure to rise above the level of wage labor upon themselves rather than upon the institutions that govern the pursuit of wealth or upon the persons who control those institutions, American society escapes the consequences of its own contradictions.

The measures by which workers try to maintain their self-regard serve in various ways to reinforce the belief that America is still a land of promise. The felt need to sustain hope for their children encourages workers to believe that there will be opportunities available to them, indeed, in some cases, that there will be even greater opportunities in the future than in the past. This belief gains particular support from the obvious and unceasingly reported progress of science and technology. For example, a machine-operator with three young children commented: "There's better opportunities now than when I started. There are more things being created, like diesel engine work, things that weren't thought of when we were children. Science is growing greater every day. Children now have a better opportunity to get in on the ground floor." In the urgent search for grounds for hope, the fact that success in new industrial fields built on scientific research requires either capital or education and training which their children may have difficulty in acquiring passes unnoticed.

If they have redefined advancement in terms closer to the realities of their own experience, workers may continue to feel that there are still real opportunities to get ahead. Security and small gains in the factory are within reach. Since Americans live on an escalator standard of living which offers an ever-growing array of things to buy and to have, there must always be new opportunities for advancement by purchase.

The social order is thus protected, however, only at the psychological expense of those who have failed. The destructive character of guilt and self-blame is obvious. But workers' attempts to avoid self-depreciation also strip much of their lives of positive significance in more subtle ways.

The justification for the universal pursuit of success has been in part the assertion that men can best realize their individual potentialities by seeking to get ahead in the world. The pursuit of success not only tests one's character, it has been argued, it also strengthens and ennobles it. Since the welfare of society rests upon the self-seeking of individuals, each man can feel that he is contributing to the progress of his country by his efforts to gain personal advancement. But the defenses which workers erect against the guilt and self-blame generated by limited aspirations and failure to get ahead tend to strip their jobs of meaning and significance and to inhibit rather than stimulate personal growth and self-development.

Both security and small goals in the factory (except for wage increases) are essentially defensive in character. The concern with security is based upon fear and uncertainty; sought-for job improvements (again except for wage increases) entail primarily escape from difficulties. As goals, therefore, they constitute patterns of avoidance rather than of creative activity. Once gained, they offer workers no positive gratifications, no meaningful experience. Some measure of security is undoubtedly necessary as the basis for the pursuit of other ends. But security, however labeled, cannot in itself substitute for the process of personal growth and enrichment which is assumed to be inherent in the pursuit of advancement.

Workers, as we have seen, also try to maintain the illusion of persisting ambition by extending the meaning of advancement to include the acquisition of personal possessions. This extension of the meaning of advancement is part of the shift from concern with getting ahead in the occupational world to concern with leisure time and leisure activities which we have noted earlier.* This changing emphasis, which plays down the values of production and stresses the values of consumption, is both a consequence and a completion of workers' alienation from their labor. Since leisure is becoming the major area of self-fulfillment, the job becomes increasingly instrumental, and workers are tied to their jobs primarily by the cash nexus. Work in the factory, as a fifty-year-old machine-operator put it, is "just bread and butter," a necessary evil to be endured because of the weekly pay check.

But men cannot spend eight hours per day, forty hours each week, in activity which lacks all but instrumental meaning. They therefore try to find some significance in the work they must do. Workers may take pride, for example, in executing skillfully even the routine tasks to which they are

---

* See p. 114.

assigned. "When I put up a pile of doors or fenders and it's a good job, I appreciate it," said a fender-wrapper. "I have an appreciation of myself when I do a good job." They may derive a moral satisfaction from doing "an honest day's work," even if they feel, as some do, that they are being exploited by management. They may try to squeeze out some sense of personal significance by identifying themselves with the product, standardized though it may be, and with the impersonal corporation in which they are anonymous, easily replaceable entities. A line repairman in his late thirties commented: "A lot of fellows like to work in the plant. They take pride in the product they turn out. A lot of them, even if they only do a little operation, they look at a finished car and seem to think they had some part in it. I've thought about that myself. I was up north fishing once and I ran into a couple of guys—I didn't know them but they work in the plant—and when we met one of them said to me, 'You an A.B.C.-maker too?' "

We know little of the deeper consequences of such makeshift substitutes for full-bodied emotional satisfaction on the job, but it does not seem likely that workers can derive much real satisfaction from these attenuated meanings in a context in which individual economic advancement is of central concern.

Since workers do not deny the validity of the tradition of opportunity or reject the legitimacy of economic or other institutions because of their inability to rise from the level of wage labor, it is easy to overlook these more subtle consequences of the disparity between tradition and reality. Lack of explicit dissatisfaction, of rebelliousness or radicalism, is taken as evidence of positive satisfaction. But not only may workers be experiencing psychological travail because of their failure, they may also be losing whatever desire they once possessed for a positive and creative work life. Chronic absence of rewarding experience, as Lewis Mumford has reminded us, produces lack of desire for such experience.

In a real sense, the idea that the goal of everyone should be unlimited personal advancement has been an historical accident. It emerged in large part because of the unusual opportunities offered in a new society which was being built across an empty continent rich in resources. But in no society is it possible for everyone to move up. In every society there must be those who perform the lesser tasks, those who "hew wood and draw water," or in an industrial society, those who man the machines. In a complex modern society, access to the top positions becomes more and more identified with extended training and unusual personal ability. To persist in the belief that everyone should strive to achieve individual economic success is to maintain values which, in some degree, are no longer appropriate.

If we are to continue to give self-development and self-fulfillment, values which underlie the belief in the desirability of universal striving for advancement, any significant content in this modern world, we must redefine them in terms of the realities of a complex industrial society. The extension of opportunities for advancement to those now laboring under disabilities not of their own making, desirable though it is, hardly touches what are perhaps the more important—and more difficult—problems: How shall we enable those who do the routine, humble tasks in our society to find meaning and satisfaction in their work? How shall we provide them with opportunities for personal growth and enrichment?

We need to explore the ways in which a complex society can solve these problems. Such an exploration might well begin with the following hypotheses suggested by some of our observations in Autotown.

As we have already seen, those men who do routine jobs will seek their major satisfactions in "the things I do when I get home from work," as one man remarked. Part of the answer to these problems, therefore, lies in the progressive enrichment of leisure activities. But we cannot deal with the problem of leisure without taking into account the nature of the work men do. The needs men try to satisfy in recreation may, in part, be generated by their experience on the job. One worker who was interviewed, for example, reported that he had usually felt it necessary to drop into a tavern for a few beers after a day spent on the assembly line; since being transferred to a job in parts and service, the after-work beer habit had disappeared. A job that leaves men physically or psychologically overfatigued, as does the assembly line, according to the consistent testimony of many workers, destroys the possibility of a lively and creative pattern of recreation.

Without more systematic analysis it is difficult to judge the adequacy of the recreational pursuits of industrial workers. The American approach to leisure, on the whole, has been casual and unorganized. The provision of opportunities for recreation has been left largely in the hands of those intent primarily on reaping a profit rather than satisfying human needs. The assertion that the businessmen of recreation are merely providing the public with what they want neglects the fact that most people, as J. L. Hammond notes in his discussion of "common enjoyment" in England, "have leisure without the tradition of leisure."[4] "The average citizen," Mannheim has said, "is unable to invent new uses for his leisure,"[5] and since he has no traditional patterns to fall back upon, he is largely dependent upon what is made available to him. In a society largely dominated by success values, many leisure pursuits, as Lundberg and his colleagues point out in their detailed study of leisure, may tend to "lose their unique and primary value as recreation and become merely another department of activity devoted to the achievement of prestige or status."[6]

Even if leisure does become the workers' major source of personal satisfaction, work, which is still the largest single activity in men's lives, cannot remain purely instrumental in character. We have already described how men try to derive a significant sense of self on their jobs by taking pride in the (standardized, mass-produced) product, in efficient (even if routine) work, and in the knowledge that they have done an "honest day's work." But these values can only become substantially rewarding if there exists a corporate purpose which gives significant meaning to their jobs. Several workers remarked approvingly, for example, that during the war "things were different. You knew what you were working for—to bring the boys back home."

Elton Mayo and his colleagues and followers have found that sense of corporate purpose in the small work group.[7] The existence of informal groups in the factory characterized by shared sentiments and stable social relationships, they have argued, provides the common values and group goals which give work and life their meaning and significance. But men need more than the satisfactions derived from predictable patterns of social interaction on the job and from working with a "good bunch of guys." They seek in their jobs to satisfy desires derived not only from their co-workers but also from family and friends and from their experience as members of the community and the larger society. If workers find it difficult to realize the values they have acquired from the larger culture, as they do in the case of success and advancement, then the solution to the problems of the meaning and purpose of their labor lies not merely in reorganization of the job situation but in changes in the values of the larger society or in institutional changes which give them a greater degree of control over their fate.

It would seem from our observations that workers have already begun, however tentatively, to shuffle the hierarchy of values which govern their behavior. In their defensive efforts to prevent frustration and self-deprecation they assign to success a less prominent, less overriding place in their scheme of things. Since the universal search for individual success can result, in our society, only in widespread failure and frustration, this is probably a desirable change in values, although it contains the danger of sharply differentiated class ideologies which would sustain and justify a rigid, highly stratified class structure.

But if workers have relegated success to a more reasonable place in their hierarchy of values, they have not given up the ideal of advancement. They have begun to redefine advancement in realistic and effective, as well as defensive, terms. They have come to see that their future well-being lies in a collective effort to achieve common goals, for example, general wage increases, rather than in the private pursuit of success. Their work in usually dead-end jobs can have new meaning if they continue to redefine advancement as a quantitative increase of things within the reach of everyone, that is, as a rise in the general standard of living, a goal achieved together rather than apart. The common good would then become an explicit aim rather than the accidental product of each individual's search for self-advancement. Changes in economic institutions and organization might be necessary to enhance workers' sense of participation in this collective effort, but the existence of a common objective would give meaning and significance to both great achievements and the faithful performance of humble tasks.

Footnotes to Chapter X

1. For an analysis of the values basic to home ownership, see J. P. Dean: *Home Ownership*, New York, Harper & Brothers, 1945, Chapter 2.
2. See "The Backward Art of Spending Money," in *The Backward Art of Spending Money and Other Essays*, New York, McGraw-Hill Book Company, Inc., 1937, pp. 3–19.
3. Dean, *op. cit.*
4. J. L. Hammond: *The Growth of Common Enjoyment*, London, Oxford University Press, 1948, L. T. Hobhouse Memorial Lecture No. 3, p. 19.
5. K. Mannheim: *Man and Society in an Age of Reconstruction*, p. 317.
6. G. Lundberg, M. Komarovsky, and M. A. McInerny: *Leisure: A Suburban Study*, New York, Columbia University Press, 1934, p. 17.
7. See E. Mayo: *Human Problems of an Industrial Civilization* and *Social Problems of an Industrial Civilization*; F. J. Roethlisberger and W. J. Dickson: *Management and the Worker*; and T. N. Whitehead: *Leadership in a Free Society*, Cambridge, Harvard University Press, 1936.

Index

"A.B.C." plant, organization of, 34–35; automotive production divisions, 35, 37, 38–39, 65–66; axle and final assembly division, 35, 65, 66, 68: *see also* assembly line, final assembly; experimental and engineering division, 35, 37, 38; inspection division, 35, 37, 38–39, 62, 68, 72: *see also* inspection, inspectors; maintenance division, 35, 36, 37, 38, 66, 68; material-handling division, 35, 36, 37, 38–39, 66, 68, 72; motor and crankshaft division, 35, 65, 68; parts and service division, 35, 36, 37–39, 66, 68, 72; sheet metal and paint division, 35, 65, 68, 69; tool and die division, 35, 37, 38.

Ability and advancement: *see* advancement and ability.

Advancement, and ability, 20–21, 40, 52–53, 55; and character, 20; and hard work, 20; collective character of, 20; in corporations, qualifications for, 6, 116; in the factory, 114, 118: *see also* foremanship, promotion; workers' definition of, 124–26, 130, 133–34.

Age, and foremanship, 45, 50, 52; and insecurity, 83; and out-of-the-shop goals, 80, 87.

Alger, Horatio, 1, 3.

Alienation, 83, 85–86.

Ambition, 6, 95, 101, 123, 130.

American Schools and Colleges Association, 1, 9.

Anderson, H. Dewey, 128.

Apprentice training, 25, 41–42, 63, 113, 115, 116.

Aspirations, and education, 48, 93; and family responsibilities, 93; and

job routines, 60, 94; and marriage, 116–17, 118; and past experience, 51; and reality, 124; chronology of, 110–22; for children, 124, 126–27, 129; limited nature of, 110; of youth, 112–15.

Assembly line, 29–30, 65, 66, 68, 70–71, 78, 79, 83, 94, 114.

Assembly line workers, 41, 70–71, 75.

Associations, membership in, and foremanship, 54–56.

Authority, attitudes toward, 59, 118.

Automobile industry, and small business, 16–17; concentration in, 16; growth of, 12–15; labor relations in, 27, 55; mechanization in, 15, 19, 34; opportunities in, 13–21; profits in, 14; skilled labor in, 19; unemployment in, 17–18, 33; wages in, 15, 17, 19, 20, 21, 34.

Bakke, E. Wight, 49n, 54n, 70n.

Beasely, Norman, 22.

Bell, Alexander Graham, 8.

Bendix, Reinhardt, 86, 95.

Bloom, G. F., 17n.

Calkins, R. D., 60.

Career pattern, 117; *see also* life plan.

Carnegie, Dale, 2, 7.

Chamberlain, Neil W., 46.

Change, resistance to, 60.

Character, and advancement, 20; and success, 7.

Chrysler, Walter, 13.

Chrysler Corporation, 16, 18.

Class ideologies, 133.

Class structure, 133.

Clerks, 36.

Cohn, David L., 22.

135